Hong Kong

MONGOLIA

JAPAN

BEIJING ●

KOREA

C H I N A

East China
Sea

HONG KONG ●

TAIWAN

Pacific Ocean

South China
Sea

PHILIPPINES

VIETNAM

DIAMOND BOOKS

This edition published 1995 by
Diamond Books
77–85 Fulham Palace Road
Hammersmith, London W6 8JB

Text: Neil Wilson
Photography: T. F. Larsen-Collinge ABIPP
Cartography: Susan Harvey
Design: Ted Carden

First published 1990

Copyright © HarperCollins*Publishers*

Printed in Italy

ISBN 0 261 66659 2

HOW TO USE THIS BOOK

The blue section provides you with an alphabetical sequence of headings, from **ART GALLERIES** to **WALKS** via **EXCURSIONS**, **RESTAURANTS**, **SHOPPING** etc. Each entry within a topic includes information on how to get there, how much it will cost you, when it will be open and what to expect. Furthermore, every page has its own map showing the position of each item and the nearest landmark. This allows you to orientate yourself quickly and easily in your new surroundings.

To find what you want to do - having dinner, visiting a museum, going for a walk or shopping for gifts - simply flick through the blue headings and take your pick!

The red section is an alphabetical list of information. It provides essential facts about places and cultural items – 'What are Walla-wallas?', 'When is the Mooncake Festival?', 'Where is Aberdeen?' – and expands on subjects touched on in the first half of the book. This section also contains practical travel information. It ranges through how to find accommodation, where to hire a car, the variety of eating places and food available, tips on health, information on money, which newspapers are available, how to find a taxi and where the Youth Hostels are. It is lively and informative and easy to use. Each band shows the first three letters of the first entry on the page. Simply flick through the bands till you find the entry you need!

All the main entries are also cross-referenced to help you find them. Names in small capitals – **CHILDREN** – tell you that there is more information about the item you are looking for under the topic on churches in the first part of the book. So when you read 'see **CHILDREN**' you turn to the blue heading for **CHILDREN**. The instruction 'see **A-Z**', after a word, lets you know that the word has its own entry in the second part of the book. Similarly words in bold type – **Lamma** – also let you know that there is an entry in the gazetteer for the indicated name. In both cases you just look under the appropriate heading in the red section.

INTRODUCTION

The view from Victoria Peak at sunset is breathtaking. Laid out at your feet is a bristling vista of skyscrapers: international banks, hotels, and corporate headquarters, lit up like space-ships along the edge of Victoria Harbour. Muffled city sounds drift up from the crowded streets below, where streams of rush-hour traffic course along the packed freeways. Night-time neons flicker into life, unrolling rippled ribbons of colour across the water: red, yellow, green, and blue. Across the harbour, beyond the sprawling roofs and streetlamps of Kowloon, the hills of China press dark against the evening sky, while the winking lights of yet another air-liner slant down towards the bright strip of Kai Tak's runway. The harbour sparkles with the glow-worm lights of a hundred anchored ships, while the Star Ferries, like fat little water-beetles, work busily back and forth.

Hong Kong is one of the most densely pop-ulated places in the world, with more than 5.6 million people squeezed into a habit-able land area of under 400 square kilome-tres. (This is roughly equivalent to the entire population of Scotland living on the Isle of Wight! The Sham Shui Po area of Kowloon holds the world record for population den-sity, at 165,000 people per square kilome-tre.) But it is also the world's second-busiest container port, its third-largest financial centre, and a major manufacturing econo-my with one of the highest growth rates in the world.

Yet if you had been able to look out from this same spot only 150 years ago, you would have seen no more than a barren, rocky island, inhabited by a handful of fishermen and farmers, and the occasional band of pirates. At that time Britain's trading interests with China were concentrated in the city of Canton (Guangzhou), where fortunes were being made illicitly by selling opium through corrupt

Chinese officials in exchange for tea, silk and porcelain. Worried by the problems of opium addiction and trade deficits, the Chinese emperor cracked down on the British merchants, besieging them in their warehouses in Canton and demanding the surrender of 20,000 chests of opium. This act sparked off a series of conflicts between Britain and China known as the Opium Wars, through which the British extracted important trading concessions from the Chinese.

The first skirmish at Canton in 1840 resulted in Britain claiming Hong Kong Island as a colony and trading post on 26 January, 1841, when the Union Jack was raised on the foreshore at Possession Point (close to present-day Possession Street). The Treaty of Nanking, in 1842, formally ceded Hong Kong Island to the British in perpetuity, and in 1860 the First Convention of Peking ceded the Kowloon Peninsula and neighbouring Stonecutter's Island. Finally, the Second Convention of Peking leased the New Territories to Britain for 99 years, commencing on 1 July, 1898.

From shaky beginnings, Hong Kong's status as a free port and its position as an entrepot for trade with China soon saw it prosper as the easternmost outpost of the British Empire. Its *laissez-faire* capitalism attracted entrepreneurs of all kinds, including many Chinese who did not mind British rule provided they were allowed to get on with the business of making a profit. The colony's population and economy grew steadily over the years, with great influxes of refugees following a series of upheavals in China: the overthrow of the Manchu dynasty in 1911; the Japanese invasion in the 1930s; and the declaration of the Communist

Republic in 1950. It was the combination of political stability, free enterprise, and cheap refugee labour that has been largely responsible for Hong Kong's economic success.

For the traveller Hong Kong offers the chance to sample a fascinating mixture of East and West, ancient and modern, exotic and familiar. This juxtaposition means that you can comfortably acclimatize to the culture shock a little at a time, retreating to the reassuring familiarity of Western-style hotels and restaurants when you want to – because for all its Westernized outward appearance, Hong Kong is an overwhelmingly Chinese city. A full 98% of the population are of Chinese origin.

Here, modern technology co-exists with the centuries-old beliefs of Taoism, Confucianism and Buddhism; business people consult fortune tellers as well as economic forecasts; high-tech buildings are sited according to the rules of 'feng shui', the ancient Chinese system of geomancy that ensures harmony between a house and the elements; huge, modern department stores sit across the street from traditional, fresh-food markets; Western-style fast-food restaurants exist alongside 'dai pai dongs' (street food stalls) serving ducks' feet and fried intestines.

So take your time and begin by getting your bearings from the top of Victoria Peak. Looking north, the skyscrapers below you form the commercial heart of Hong Kong – the area is officially named Victoria, but known to everyone as Central. Across the crowded harbour is the Kowloon peninsula, with its many hotels and shopping centres, and beyond that the mostly rural New Territories stretch north to the Chinese border. In

the opposite direction lie the boat yards and floating restaurants of
Aberdeen, the watery thrills of Ocean Park, the sandy beaches of
Repulse and Deep Water Bays, and the little market town of Stanley.
Beyond is the outline of Lamma Island, while off to the west are Lantau
Island, and, on a clear day, distant Macau.

Take a sightseeing trip on the top deck of a rattling Hong Kong tram,
out to Kennedy Town and back. Stop on the return trip to delve into the
back streets of Western District, where the essential 'Chineseness' of
Hong Kong is strongly felt. Here you will find shops dealing in ginseng,
ground deer antler, snake blood and other exotic medicines; pungent
dried-food stores, with colourful mounds of orange shrimps, black
mushrooms, and flattened squid, and shelves of sharks' fins and birds'
nests; grisly butcher shops, with their traditional red lights, festooned
with all kinds of gory offal; street vendors offering snacks of fried chick-
ens' feet, and workshops turning out elaborate Chinese coffins.

Cross the harbour by Star Ferry to hunt for bargains in neon-lit Nathan
Road and the busy shopping streets of Tsim Sha Tsui. Take afternoon tea
in the stylish Peninsula Hotel, or stroll along the new promenade
admiring the views across the harbour to the skyscrapers lining the
waterfront of Central and Wan Chai. Then, in the evening, you might
explore the side streets around Temple Street night market, and if you
look beyond the main area selling jeans, t-shirts, cassettes and watches,

you will find little stalls offering everything from coin collections and jade jewellery to posters of pop stars. The seafood 'dai pai dongs' here offer a colourful selection of live dinners; pick a dish – from commonplace clams and prawns to exotic mantis shrimp or horseshoe crab – and it is quickly cooked and served on a rickety table on the pavement. Make the effort to visit the New Territories, where you will see another side of Hong Kong: the new towns with their factories and apartment blocks, which are the basis of the colony's manu-facturing wealth; and traditional farms and fishing villages which still follow a rural life style stem-ming from pre-colonial days. Or take a hydrofoil to Macau, with its Portuguese heritage, sleepy backstreets, and brash waterfront casinos. And if political condi-tions permit, make the journey to  Guangzhou, the city where Hong Kong's story began, and now looks likely to end.

Following two years of talks, Britain agreed, in 1984, to hand over to China all of Hong Kong – including Hong Kong Island and Kowloon, which could not function economically without the hinterland of the New Territories – at midnight on 30 June, 1997. In theory, the agree-ment allows Hong Kong to continue with its present social, legal and economic systems for 50 years as a Special Administrative Region of Guangdong Province. But the events of Tiananmen Square in 1989 left the majority of Hong Kong's people with little confidence in the promises of China's leaders, and many are making plans to leave. The sun is finally setting on this last remnant of the British Empire, and the view from The Peak is shadowed with uncertainty. Enjoy it while you can.

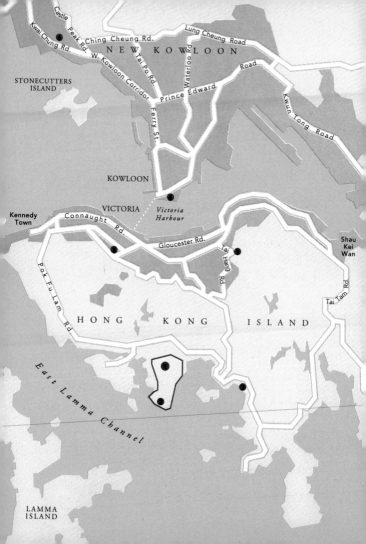

1.OCEAN PARK Wong Chuk Hang, HK.
❑ 1000-1800. Ocean Park Citybus from MTR Admiralty. ❑ HK$100/50
(HK$112/58 including Citybus return fare).
Huge theme park on the south of the island, with a roller coaster, cable cars, an oceanarium, performing dolphins and killer whales.

2.WATER WORLD Adjacent to Ocean Park.
❑ 1000-1700 May-Oct. Ocean Park Citybus from MTR Admiralty.
❑ HK$45/15 (HK$57/23 including Citybus return fare).
Assorted swimming and diving pools, a wave pool, and five water slides.

3.AW BOON HAW (TIGER BALM) GARDENS Tai Hang Rd, Tai Hang, HK.
❑ 1000-1600. Bus 11. ❑ Free.
Brightly-painted plaster grottoes, tableaux and sculptures portraying Chinese gods, myths and folk tales. Great fun. See PARKS & GARDENS.

4.HONG KONG SPACE MUSEUM 10 Salisbury Rd, Tsim Sha Tsui, Kowloon.
❑ 1400-2130 Mon., Wed.-Fri., 1300-2130 Sat., 1030-2130 Sun. Star Ferry; MTR to Tsim Sha Tsui. ❑ Museum free; Space Theatre HK$15/10
Lots of 'hands-on' exhibits to keep children busy.

5.ZOOLOGICAL & BOTANICAL GARDENS Upper Albert Rd, Central, HK.
❑ 0630-1900. Bus 3 from Connaught Centre. ❑ Free.
Small, pretty zoo with some interesting animals. See PARKS & GARDENS.

6.LAI CHI KOK AMUSEMENT PARK Lai Wan Rd, Lai Chi Kok, Kowloon.
❑ 1100-2300. MTR to Mei Foo. ❑ HK$5/3.
Dodgems, fairground rides, pinball machines, miniature zoo, etc.

7.REPULSE BAY BEACH Repulse Bay, HK.
Bus 6, 61.
A pleasant, sandy, and very popular stretch of beach. See **A-Z**.

1.CENTRAL MTR to Central; Star Ferry; tram.
Officially named Victoria, but everyone calls it Central. The government and business centre of the city, featuring many spectacular skyscrapers.

2.WESTERN MTR to Sheung Wan; tram.
Stretching west from Central, this is a very Chinese area. The streets are lined with charming traditional shops and businesses. See **WALK 2.**

3.WAN CHAI MTR to Wan Chai; tram.
To the east of Central, this is an area of neon-lit nightclubs, Chinese restaurants, seedy topless bars, and British-style pubs. It was the setting for Richard Mason's novel The World of Suzie Wong. *See* **WALK 3.**

4.CAUSEWAY BAY MTR to Causeway Bay; tram.
Busy district of smart shops, restaurants, cinemas and nightclubs, and the site of the Royal HK Yacht Club and the famous Noonday Gun.

5.THE PEAK Peak Tram.
Rising to 554 m, this is Hong Kong's most exclusive residential area. A trip up The Peak is a must for all visitors – the panorama of the city and the harbour is breathtaking, especially in the evening.

6.MID LEVELS Bus 12 from Connaught Centre.
A residential area between Central-Western and the Peak, notable for its fine colonial architecture. Also the site of Hong Kong University.

7.TSIM SHA TSUI MTR to Tsim Sha Tsui; Star Ferry.
Situated around the 'Golden Mile' of Nathan Road, this is the colony's principal hotel and shopping area. It contains Asia's largest shopping centre (Harbour City - see **SHOPPING 2**), *and the terminus of the Kowloon-Canton Railway.*

8.YAU MA TEI MTR to Jordan, MTR to Yau Ma Tei.
This old Chinese commercial and residential area, lying to the north of Tsim Sha Tsui, is well known for its jade market (see **MARKETS**) *and lively night markets, fortune-tellers and street entertainers.*

Island

Eastern Corridor

Hing Fat St.

Causeway Road

VICTORIA PARK

Yee Wo St.

Gloucester Road

Hung Hing Rd.

Hennessy Rd.

Johnston

Cheong Wan Rd

Gascoigne Rd

Jordan Road

Austin Road

Chatham Road

Nathan Road

Salisbury Road

Canton Rd.

Victoria Harbour

Harcourt Road

Queensway

Drake Street

Cotton

Garden Rd.

Peak Tram

Central

Star Ferry

Connaught Road Central

Queen's Road Central

Queen's St.

Apperbury St.

Caine Rd.

Robinson Rd.

Wellington St.

Draguien St.

Wyndham Street

Lower Albert Rd.

Wyndham Street

Arbuthnot Road

1.HONG KONG ACADEMY OF PERFORMING ARTS
1 Gloucester Rd, Wan Chai, HK, tel: 5-8231500.
Bus 21; Star Ferry to Wan Chai.
This is Hong Kong's premier arts venue. It includes the Concert Hall, Recital Hall, Lyric Theatre, Drama Theatre, Studio Theatre and Open-air Theatre.

2.HONG KONG ARTS CENTRE 2 Harbour Rd, Wan Chai, HK, tel: 5-8230200. Bus 21; Star Ferry to Wan Chai.
Three theatres regularly holding concerts, plays, recitals, films, etc.

3.CITY HALL Low Block, Edinburgh Pl., Central, HK, tel: 5-739595.
Star Ferry; MTR to Central.
Contains a 1500-seat auditorium, a theatre and recital hall, with a programme of classical music, recitals, and occasionally drama and ballet.

4.HONG KONG COLISEUM Salisbury Rd, Tsim Sha Tsui East, Kowloon, tel: 3-7659233. Star Ferry to Hung Hom.
This modern 12,500-seat stadium is the setting for sporting events, ballets, ice shows, and orchestral and rock concerts.

5.FRINGE CLUB 2 Lower Albert Rd, Central, HK, tel: 5-217251.
MTR to Central; tram.
❏ Membership HK$10 per night, HK$30 per month.
Jazz, comedy, avant-garde dance and drama.

6.COLUMBIA CLASSIC Great Eagle Centre, 23 Harbour Centre, Wan Chai, HK, tel: 5-738291.
Bus 21; Star Ferry to Wan Chai. ❏ HK$25-30.
One of Hong Kong's better cinemas, with a good programme of quality Western, Chinese and Japanese films.

7.HILTON HOTEL 2 Queen's Rd, Central, HK, tel: 5-233111, ext. 2009. MTR to Central; tram; Star Ferry.
Regularly stages 'dinner theatre' which is generally a light comedy featuring visiting British companies. Should be booked well in advance.

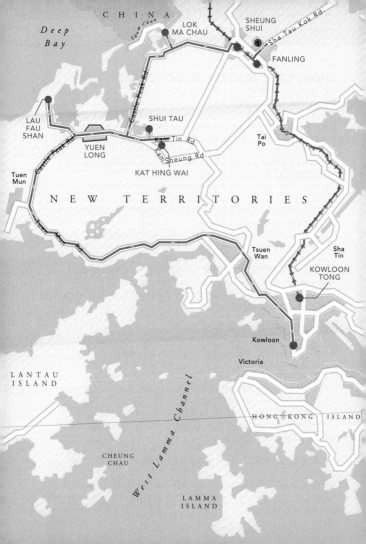

New Territories

*A one-day excursion to the New Territories (see **A-Z**).*

Take the MTR (see **A-Z**) to Kowloon Tong, then the KCR (see **A-Z**) to Fanling. From the station, walk into town along Sha Tau Kok Road. Past the open-air market in the playground to the left, you will see the main entrance to Luen Wo Market (1). (To save yourself this 15 minute walk you can take bus 78K from the station and get off at the stop in front of the market.) This is a typical New Territories market, selling fresh fruit and vegetables, fish, meat, and other day-to-day necessities with vendors adding up prices on an abacus. Look out for stalls selling Chinese teas, live pigeons, quails and turtles, exotic fruits like lychees and longans (similar to but smaller than lychees, with juicy white flesh and a single seed), cakes of white tofu (soya-bean curd), and paper offerings (models of cars, houses, TV sets, etc. which are burnt in order to ascend to dead ancestors and help them lead a more comfortable after-

life). On the street behind the market is a traditional herbalist's shop selling herbs, roots, leaves, seeds and exotic substances such as antler velvet from deer and

dried sea horses. The market is open from around 0900-1800, but try to get there before noon when it is at its busiest.

Return to the KCR station and take the train to the next station, Sheung Shui. From the bus terminus beside the station catch bus 76K to Yuen Long. After about 5 km you will pass a road on the right signposted for Lok Ma Chau. You can get off here and walk down the road for about 20 min to reach the once famous lookout point where tourists came to peer over the border into mysterious China, on the far side of the Shum Chun River. At Yuen Long, change to bus 54 which will take you to the walled villages of Kam Tin a few kilometres to the east. Get off at Kat Hing Wai on the right side of the main road. The village dates from the 17thC and is completely surrounded by thick brick walls, with watch-towers at the corners and archers' slit windows, built as protection from raiding pirates and brigands. There is only one narrow entrance which opens onto a single main street (lined with souvenir stalls) and has narrow alleys leading off. Hakka women (see **Hakka People**) sit at the gate, wearing traditional black tunics and black-fringed hats, and expect to be paid HK$1-2 for having their photograph taken. A less touristy and more interesting walled village is Shui Tau (walk back towards Yuen Long and turn right just after the junction with Kam Sheung Road; it takes about 15 min to reach the village).

Catch bus 54 back to Yuen Long, then bus 655 to Lau Fau Shan. Situated on a spit of land between Deep Bay, to the west, and acres of fish ponds and oyster beds, to the east, this village is famous for its seafood market and restaurants, but especially for its oysters. The area is littered with heaps of discarded oyster shells (most of the contents of which have gone to make oyster sauce) and dotted with fish and duck farms. You can buy fresh seafood from the market and take it to one of the restaurants to be cooked. Take bus 655 back to Yuen Long, and then return to the city on bus 68X to Jordan Road Bus Terminal (Kowloon), and the MTR to Central.

Avda do Coronel Mesquita

Avda do Ouvidor Xavier

Avda Horta E Costa

R. de Francisco Xavier

R. do Almirante Costa Cabral

Estrada do Respouso

Avda do Conselheiro Ferreira de Almeida

Estrada da Vitória

do Patane

R. da Ribeira

R. d. B. Carneiro

Rua do Campo

Avda do Dr. R. Rodrigues

Avda da Amizade

R. d. Felicidade

Largo
Pedro

Calçada de Barra

Paulino

República

Macau

*A one-day excursion to the Portuguese colony of Macau (see **A-Z**).*

Take the MTR (see **A-Z**) to Sheung Wan, then a hydrofoil or jetfoil from Macau Ferry Terminal (see **Macau**). After clearing customs at Macau, take bus 3 or 3A, or a taxi or pedicab (trishaw) to the Lisboa Hotel (1). This architectural monstrosity, with its ornate balconies and roulette-wheel roof, houses the busiest of Macau's six casinos, and is one of the territory's best-known landmarks. From the square, the roller-coaster hump of the Taipa Bridge (2) arches over to Taipa Island. Stroll along the waterfront on the Avenida Doutor Mario Soares and then turn left along the tree-lined Rua da Praia Grande to reach the pastel pink-and-white mansion of Government House (3) (built 1849). Continue along the promenade, past people fishing from the sea wall, and you come to Henri's Gallery (4), an excellent restaurant. Just past this, turn right uphill, then go left past the entrance to the mansion and gardens of the Governor's Residence (5) and follow the road round to the right to reach the entrance to the Bishop's Palace and Penha Chapel (6). These are not open to the public, but the grounds offer a superb view of

the Pearl River estuary, and there is a replica of the Grotto of Lourdes. From the exit, turn right and then right again to arrive at the grand old Bela Vista Hotel (7). Built at the end of the 19thC, it is a little worn around the edges, but has a charming old-world atmosphere. Stop for tea or a drink on the balcony overlooking the harbour.

Return to the waterfront and follow the road round the southern tip of Macau's peninsula, where you will find the Pousada de Sao Tiago Hotel (8) built into the foundations of a ruined 17thC fortress. It has been beautifully designed to blend in with both the ruins and the natural features of the hillside, and it's well worth pausing to have a look around. On the west side of the peninsula is the A-Ma Temple (9) (also called Ma Kok Miu) dating from the early 16thC, which is dedicated to the goddess A-Ma (known in Hong Kong as Tin Hau), protector of fishermen. She also inadvertently gave her name to the territory: one of the local Chinese names for the area was A-Ma Gau (Bay of A-Ma), which was corrupted to Macau by the Portuguese. At the point where the road meets the waterfront again you will find the popular Maritime Museum (10) (1000-1800 Wed.-Mon.; free) which charts the voyages of Chinese

and Portuguese explorers, and has some interesting historic vessels moored at the neighbouring wharf. Continue along the Rua do Almirante Sergio, past ramshackle warehouses and workshops, shacks and shipping offices, to where the floating Palace Casino (11) is moored (looking rather down-at-heel these days). Just beyond it turn right into Avenida de Almeida Ribiero (with the Grand Hotel on the corner) which is Macau's main street. A short distance before the main square (Largo do Senado) there is a lane (Pateo do Cotovelo), on the right, where you will find the Café Safari (12), a traditional coffee house and an excellent spot for a lunch of *caldo verde* (green vegetable soup) and roast sardines.

Wander through the European-style square in front of the late-18thC Leal Senado (Senate Building) (13), with its 1876 facade, past the lunchtime crowds gathered round the fountain, to the ruins of Sao Paolo (14). The beautiful and ornate facade is all that remains of a magnificent 17thC cathedral which was destroyed by fire in 1835. Up the hill to the right of Sao Paolo is the 17thC Monte Fortress (15) with its old cannons pointing out over the harbour. These were the very guns used to repel the attempted Dutch invasion of 1622. Go back down to Sao Paolo, down the steps on the north side, left along the narrow cobbled street, and down the stairs at the end to find the Luis de Camoes Gardens (16) to the right. The gardens are pleasant for strolling, and you will see people walking here with their caged songbirds, or huddled over games of checkers. Portugal's greatest poet, Camoes (1524-1580), claimed that he wrote his epic *Os Lusiadas* here. Beside the park is an impressive colonial building dating from the 1770s. At one time it was the Macau office of the British East India Company, and until recently it was the Camoes Museum (17) (at the time of writing it is undergoing renovation). Here too is the old Protestant Cemetery (18), containing the graves of many British and American clergymen, military personnel, merchants and seamen. Wander back to the main square where you might like to have dinner at the 80-year-old Fat Sui Lau Restaurant (19) on the Rua da Felicidade before heading for the ferry pier (20) and the jetfoil back to Hong Kong.

EXCURSION 3

Guangzhou

A one-day, and overnight, excursion to the Chinese city of Guangzhou, which gives the independent traveller a chance to see something of the city without the trouble or expense of finding hotel accommodation.

Catch the morning train from Kowloon to Guangzhou (see **A-Z**). From the station you can travel to the sights by taxi, although a keen walker can easily take in the attractions lying along Jie Fang Lu between the railway station and the river (a walk of about 8 km). Nearest to the station is Yue Xiu Park (1) where you will find the Zhenhai Tower (2), built in 1380 during the Ming Dynasty as part of the city wall and now housing the Municipal Museum. Nearby are the statue of the Five Rams (3), the civic symbol of Guangzhou, and the Dr Sun Yat-Sen Monument (4). Downhill from the monument is the Dr Sun Yat-Sen Memorial Hall (5) which was built in 1925 in honour of the founder of the People's Republic of China. Down a side street on the other side of Jie Fang Lu is situated the Temple of the Six Banyans (6), with its 6thC, 55 m-high Flower Pagoda, home of the Guangzhou Buddhist Association. Farther south is the 7thC Huaisheng Mosque (7), thought to have been founded by the first Moslem missionary to China in AD 627.

At the end of Jie Fang Lu go right along Yi De Lu, passing the Roman Catholic cathedral (8) completed in 1888, then turn left onto Ren Min Lu to reach the river. Walk right along the river bank and across a small bridge onto Shamian Island. This was where European traders built their warehouses and mansions in the 19thC, most of which have been converted into offices and apartments. The island is something of a tourist centre now: housing the huge, modern White Swan Hotel (9) and a number of Western-style shops and restaurants. Across the canal on the north side of the island is the fascinating Qing Ping Market (10). The opportunity to wander through its bustling alleys should not be missed. Here you will see all kinds of things for sale: from live lizards and monkeys to dried sea horses and starfish, snakes, songbirds, eels, turtles, frogs, salamanders and goldfish. There are also stalls selling pottery, jewellery, pots and pans, and other household items.

Among the sights lying well outside walking distance are the Peasant Movement Institute (11), founded in 1924 in a Confucian temple and used by the Communist Party as a place to train peasant leaders

(Mao Zedong and Zhou En-lai both lectured here); the Memorial Garden to the Martyrs (12), commemorating the 1927 Communist uprising; the Mausoleum of the 72 Martyrs (13), built in memory of those who fell in the unsuccessful Canton insurrection of 1911; and the Canton Zoo (14), founded in 1958 on the outskirts of the city and one of the biggest and best zoos in China (the pandas are, of course, the main attraction).

From Shamian Island, cross the Zhu Jiang (Pearl River) by Renmin Bridge, keeping on the right side of the street, and turn right at Houde Lu. This leads past a market to the ticket office and embarkation compound for the overnight boat (see **Guangzhou**) which plies downriver to Hong Kong.

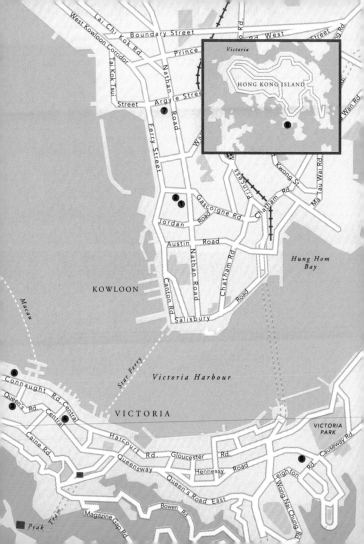

MARKETS

1.TEMPLE STREET Temple St, Yau Ma Tei, Kowloon.
❏ 2000-2300. MTR Jordan.
Lively night market with goods at bargain prices. See **MUSTS, Eating Out.**

2.JADE MARKET Kansu & Battery Sts, Yau Ma Tei, Kowloon.
❏ 1000-1530. MTR Jordan.
*Over 400 stalls dealing in jade of all shapes and shades. Don't buy any-
thing expensive unless you know what you're doing.*

3.CAT STREET Upper Lascar Row, Sheung Wan, HK.
❏ approximately 1000-1800. MTR Sheung Wan; tram.
*Flea market selling all kinds of junk, from coins, stamps, and badges to
teapots, penknives and second-hand typewriters. See* **WALK 2**.

4.THE LANES Between Queen's & Des Voeux Rds, Central, HK.
❏ approximately 1000-1800. MTR Central; tram.
*Two narrow alleys packed with stalls specializing in bargain fashions,
handbags, jewellery and accessories.*

5.JARDINE'S BAZAAR Jardine's Bazaar, Causeway Bay, HK.
❏ approximately 0800-2100. MTR Causeway Bay; tram.
*Fruit and vegetable market standing side-by-side with a bazaar selling
inexpensive clothing, sportswear and accessories.*

6.POOR MAN'S NIGHTCLUB Beside HK-China Ferry Terminal,
Sheung Wan, HK.
❏ 1830-0100. MTR Sheung Wan; tram.
Inexpensive clothes, records, cassettes, watches, electronic gadgets, etc.

7.BIRD MARKET Hong Lok St, Yau Ma Tei, Kowloon.
❏ approximately 0800-1200. MTR Mong Kok.
Fascinating market selling songbirds and beautiful bamboo cages.

8.STANLEY MARKET Stanley Market Rd, Stanley, HK.
❏ 1000-1900. Bus 6, 260.
Bargains in casual wear, leather, silk items, household goods, souvenirs.

Victoria Harbour

Star Ferry

Victoria Harbour

VICTORIA PARK

Eastern Corridor

Hing Fat St.

Island

Causeway Bay Road

Yee Wo St.

Gloucester Road

Hung Hing Rd.

Hennessy Rd.

Harcourt Road

Queensway

Tree Drive

Garden Rd.

Cotton

Peak Tram

Central

Connaught Road Central

Queen's Road Central

Aberdeen St.

Caine Rd.

Robinson Rd.

Cheong Wan Rd

Chatham Road

Gascoigne Rd.

Kowloon Park Rd.

Jordan Road

Austin Road

Nathan Road

Salisbury Road

Canton Rd.

West

West

Connaught Road

Des Voeux Road

Queen's Road

Pottinger Rd.

Pok Fu Lam Rd.

Whitty St.

1.HONG KONG MUSEUM OF ART 10&11/F, High Block, City Hall, Connaught Rd, HK.
❏ 1000-1800 Mon.-Wed., Fri., Sat., 1300-1800 Sun.
Star Ferry; MTR Central. ❏ Free.
Interesting collection of Chinese antiquities, paintings and calligraphy from the 17th-early 20thC.

2.HONG KONG MUSEUM OF HISTORY Kowloon Park, Haiphong Rd, Tsim Sha Tsui, Kowloon.
❏ 1000-1800 Mon.-Thu., Sat., 1300-1800 Sun.
MTR Tsim Sha Tsui. ❏ Free.
A record of Hong Kong's history, archaeology, and culture. Includes a large collection of early photographs of the colony.

3.FLAGSTAFF HOUSE MUSEUM OF TEA WARE Victoria Barracks, Cotton Tree Dr., Central, HK.
❏ 1000-1700 Thu.-Tue. Bus 3, 12, 23, 40, 103; tram. ❏ Free.
Tea ware, mostly Chinese and dating from the Western Zhou Dynasty to the present, housed in Hong Kong's oldest Western-style building (1845).

4.FUNG PING SHAN MUSEUM University of Hong Kong, 94 Bonham Rd, Western, HK.
❏ 0930-1800 Mon.-Sat. Bus 40M from MTR Admiralty. ❏ Free.
Beautiful collection of early Chinese art – mostly ceramics and bronzes, but includes paintings from the Ming and Qing dynasties.

5.SAM TUNG UK MUSEUM Kwu Uk Lane, Tsuen Wan, New Terr. ❏ 0900-1600 Wed.-Mon. MTR Tsuen Wan. ❏ Free.
*Restored 18thC Hakka walled village containing exhibits of traditional furniture and farming equipment (see **Hakka People**).*

6.MUSEUM OF CHINESE HISTORICAL RELICS 1/F, Causeway Centre, 28 Harbour Rd, Wan Chai, HK.
❏ 1000-1700 Mon.-Fri., 0930-1300 Sat. Bus 10A, 20, 21, 103, 104.
❏ Free.
Changing exhibitions of Chinese paintings and handicrafts.

NEW KOWLOON

Castle Peak Rd.

Kwai Chung Rd.

Ching Cheung Rd.

Lung Cheung Road

W. Kowloon Corridor

Tai Po Rd.

Waterloo

Prince Edward

Road

Ferry St.

Kwun Tong Road

STONECUTTERS
ISLAND

KOWLOON

VICTORIA

Victoria
Harbour

Kennedy
Town

Connaught Rd.

Gloucester Rd.

Sha
Kei
Wa

Pok Fu Lam Rd.

Tai Hang Rd.

Tai Tam Rd.

HONG   KONG   ISLAND

East Lamma Channel

LAMMA
ISLAND

1.THE PEAK Victoria Peak, HK.
❏ Peak Tram 0700-0000. Free shuttle bus from Star Ferry terminal to the lower tram terminus. ❏ HK$10 return.
Take a cool, evening walk around The Peak, followed by dinner in the Peak Tower while enjoying the dazzling views of the city lights below.
See **CITY DISTRICTS, WALK 1.**

2.STAR FERRY Tsim Sha Tsui, Kowloon/ Central, HK.
❏ 0630-2330. MTR to Tsim Sha Tsui/ MTR to Central.
❏ HK$0.80 upper deck, HK$0.60 lower deck.
The seven-minute trip across spectacular Victoria Harbour in one of these venerable green-and-white vessels is a delight.

3.TEMPLE STREET NIGHT MARKET Temple Street, Yau Ma Tei, Kowloon.
❏ 2000-2300. MTR to Jordan.
Plunge into the crowds milling through brightly-lit back streets crammed with stalls selling bargains, and then sit down for a meal of clam stew at one of the sizzling seafood dai pai dongs. See **MARKETS, Eating out**.

4.HONG KONG TRAM Shau Kei Wan to Kennedy Town.
❏ 0540-0100. MTR to Central. ❏ Flat fare HK$0.60.
Grab a tram that's headed for Kennedy Town and sit upstairs at the front to enjoy the sights of Western District (see **CITY DISTRICTS**). *See* **Trams**.

5.MAN FAT SZE TEMPLE (TEMPLE OF 10,000 BUD-DHAS) Tai Po Rd, Sha Tin, New Terr.
❏ 0730-1830. MTR to Kowloon Tong, then KCR to Sha Tin.
The steep climb to this temple, in the countryside north of the city, is well worth the effort to see the 12,800 clay Buddhas and the gilded, mummi-fied remains of the temple's founder, Yuet Kai. See **TEMPLES, A-Z**.

6.THE PENINSULA HOTEL Salisbury Rd, Tsim Sha Tsui, Kowloon.
Star Ferry; MTR Tsim Sha Tsui. ❏ Around HK$50.
Linger over afternoon tea in the splendid, marble-floored, gilt-corniced lobby of 'The Pen', the grand old dame of Hong Kong's hotels.

1.CANTON 161-163 World Finance Centre North Tower, Harbour City, Tsim Sha Tsui, Kowloon.
❑ 2100-0300 Sun.-Thu., 2100-0400 Fri., Sat. MTR Tsim Sha Tsui; Star Ferry. ❑ HK$77-88 (includes two drinks).
HK's biggest and most sophisticated disco. The clientele is young and chic, a mixture of Chinese and expats. 'Top 40' music and videos.

2.NINETEEN 97 Upper G/F, 8-11 Lan Kwai Fong, Central, HK.
❑ 1100-0200. MTR Central.
An intimate and relaxed atmosphere pervades this bar and restaurant. The crowded Club 97 disco is in the same building (1000-0400).

3.KANGAROO PUB 15 Chatham Rd, Tsim Sha Tsui, Kowloon.
❑ 0800-0200. MTR Tsim Sha Tsui.
This bright, friendly, Aussie-style pub attracts a mixed crowd.

4.SKY LOUNGE Penthouse, Sheraton Hotel & Towers, 20 Nathan Rd, Tsim Sha Tsui, Kowloon.
❑ 1500-0100. MTR Tsim Sha Tsui.
Quiet, elegant lounge bar offering views over the harbour and the city's twinkling lights. Live piano music in the early evening (1630-1930).

5.CALIFORNIA 24-26 Lan Kwai Fong, Central, HK.
❑ 1200-0300 (until 0400 Fri., Sat.). MTR Central; tram.
Trendy American-style cocktail bar and restaurant, fashionable crowd. Disco for members only (from 2200; buy a membership at the door).

6.DICKENS BAR Lower G/F, Excelsior Hotel, 281 Gloucester Rd, Causeway Bay, HK.
❑ 1100-0200.
Lively pub offering English beer – a popular late-night meeting place.

7.BOTTOMS UP 4-16 Hankow Rd, Tsim Sha Tsui, Kowloon.
❑ 1600-0300. MTR to Tsim Sha Tsui. ❑ HK$25 per drink.
The most 'respectable' of Hong Kong's topless bars. The varied clientele includes women and couples.

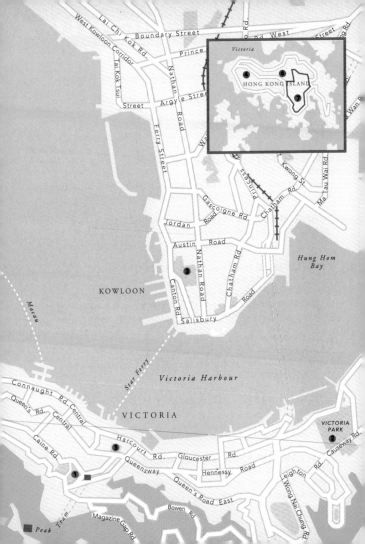

PARKS & GARDENS

1.ZOOLOGICAL & BOTANICAL GARDENS Upper Albert Rd, Central, HK.
❑ 0630-1900. Bus 3 from Connaught Centre. ❑ Free.
Pleasant landscaped gardens with good views of Government House (see A-Z) and the city. It is at its best in spring when the azaleas are in bloom.

2.VICTORIA PARK Victoria Park Rd, Causeway Bay, HK.
❑ Dawn-dusk. MTR Causeway Bay; tram. ❑ Free.
Lawns, flower beds, a swimming pool, tennis courts and a go-kart track. There is a lantern carnival here in the autumn (see Events).

3.KOWLOON PARK Nathan Rd, Tsim Sha Tsui, Kowloon.
❑ Dawn-dusk. MTR Tsim Sha Tsui. ❑ Free.
A quiet place in which to escape the bustle of Nathan Road. Features a Chinese Garden with a lotus pond and an aviary.

4.VICTORIA PEAK GARDEN Mt Austin Rd, Victoria Peak, HK.
❑ 24 hr. Peak Tram, then 15 min walk. ❑ Free.
Gardens with walkways, picnic areas and terrific views, lying just below the summit of The Peak (see CITY DISTRICTS, MUSTS). See WALK 1.

5.CHATER GARDEN Chater Rd, Central, HK.
❑ 24 hr. MTR Central; Star Ferry; tram. ❑ Free.
An oasis in the heart of the city, which is popular at lunchtimes.

6.AW BOON HAW (TIGER BALM) GARDENS Tai Hang Rd, Tai Hang, HK.
❑ 1000-1600. Bus 11. ❑ Free.
A colourful hillside maze of pathways, steps, pagodas and grottoes illustrating the world of Chinese mythology. See CHILDREN.

7.TAI TAM COUNTRY PARK South side Hong Kong Island.
❑ 24 hr. Bus 6, 260 to Stanley, then bus 14 to Tai Tam Reservoir.
❑ Free.
Wild, beautiful scenery surrounding a reservoir in the hills.

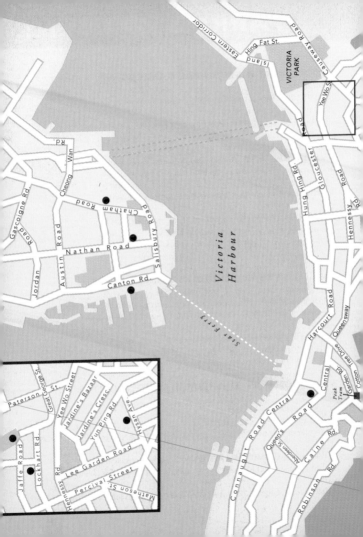

Victoria Harbour

Star Ferry

VICTORIA PARK

Eastern Corridor

Hing Fat St.

Causeway Road

Yee Wo St

Gloucester Road

Hung Hing Rd

Hennessy Rd

Harcourt Road

Queensway

Tree Drive

Central

Park Tram

Connaught Road Central

Queen's Road

Caine Rd

Robinson Rd

Aberdeen St.

Garden Rd

Cheong Wan Rd

Gascoigne Rd

Rosmead Rd

Chatham Road

Nathan Road

Salisbury Road

Canton Rd

Austin Road

Jordan

Paterson St.

Great George St.

Yee Wo Street

Jardine's Bazaar

Jardine's Cresc.

Yun Ping Rd

Yee Wo Ave.

Jaffe Road

Lockhart Rd

Hennessy Rd

Lee Garden Road

Percival Street

Matheson St.

1.JADE GARDEN 1/F, Swire House, Chater Rd, Central, HK, tel: 5-23966. MTR to Central; tram. ❑ Expensive.
Extensive range of imaginative dishes. Special set menus for tourists.

2.SUN TUNG LOK SHARK'S FIN G/F Harbour City, 25-27 Canton Rd, Tsim Sha Tsui, Kowloon, tel: 3-7220288. Star Ferry; MTR to Tsim Sha Tsui. ❑ Expensive.
Shark's fin cooked every which way. You can also try ablone, clams or many other of the delicious seafood dishes on offer.

3.NORTH SEA FISHING VILLAGE B/F, Auto Plaza, Tsim Sha Tsui East, Kowloon, tel: 3-7236843.
MTR to Tsim Sha Tsui. ❑ Expensive.
Huge restaurant serving all manner of seafood: fish, prawns, lobster, octopus, squid, shark's fin, ablone and even frog!

4.LOONG YUEN Holiday Inn Golden Mile, 50 Nathan Rd, Tsim Sha Tsui, Kowloon, tel: 3-7396268. MTR to Tsim Sha Tsui. ❑ Expensive.
Modern decor, relaxed atmosphere, efficient and helpful waiters – a good place for an introduction to a Cantonese menu.

5.FOOK LAM MOON 459 Lockhart Rd, Causeway Bay, HK, tel: 5-8912639. MTR to Causeway Bay; tram. ❑ Expensive.
Lemon chicken, crab dishes, superb abalone (but expensive, as always).

6.MAXIM'S PALACE 1/F, World Trade Centre, Causeway Bay, HK, tel: 5-760288. MTR to Causeway Bay; tram. ❑ Moderate.
Traditional Hong Kong restaurant. Serves everything from basic fare to an Imperial Banquet with camel's hump, bear's paw, elephant's trunk and 'essence of tiger'!

7.RAINBOW ROOM 22/F, Lee Gardens Hotel, Hysan Ave, Causeway Bay, HK, tel: 5-8953311, ext. 2439.
MTR to Causeway Bay; tram. ❑ Expensive.
A high ceiling, mirrors, Chinese lanterns and superb views make this one of the most beautiful restaurants in Hong Kong. Try to get a window table.

1.**CHIU CHOW GARDEN** 1 & 2/F, Hennessy Centre, 500 Hennessy Rd, Causeway Bay, HK, tel: 5-773391.
MTR to Causeway Bay; tram. ❑ Expensive.
*Traditional chiu chow dishes, including 'Iron Buddha' tea (see **Food**).*

2.**PEKING GARDEN** B/F, Alexandra House, Des Voeux Rd, Central, HK, tel: 5-266456. MTR Central; Star Ferry; tram. ❑ Expensive.
Full of tourists, but the food is good. Watch the noodle-making display.

3.**PEP'N'CHILLI** 12 Blue Pool Rd, Happy Valley, HK, tel: 5-738251.
Tram. ❑ Expensive-moderate.
Popular with expats. Try the hot and sour seafood soup (comes in an earthenware pot) and the lobster with chilli and garlic sauce.

4.**GREAT SHANGHAI** 26 Prat Ave, Tsim Sha Tsui, Kowloon, tel: 3-668158. MTR to Tsim Sha Tsui. ❑ Moderate.
Basic decor, but great food. Specialities are Peking Duck and Beggar's Chicken, plus more exotic dishes like turtle with sugar candy.

5.**UNIVERSAL CHIU CHOW** 6-8 Hysan Ave, Causeway Bay, HK, tel: 5-762727. MTR to Causeway Bay; tram. ❑ Expensive.
Pleasant and modern. Try woo tou – fish, flavoured with salted lemon or garlic and black bean sauce, dished up on a burner at your table.

6.**AMERICAN PEKING** 20 Lockhart Rd, Wan Chai, HK, tel: 5-277277. Tram; MTR to Admiralty. ❑ Inexpensive.
Excellent Peking Duck and Beggar's Chicken at reasonable prices.

7.**SHANGHAI GARDEN** 1/F, Hutchison House, Murray Rd, Central, HK, tel: 5-248181. Star Ferry. ❑ Expensive.
Good place to sample a wide range of Chinese cuisines for the first time.

8.**SZECHUAN LAU** 466 Lockhart Rd, Causeway Bay, HK, tel: 5-8919027. MTR to Causeway Bay; tram. ❑ Expensive.
Spicy Szechuan dishes, including crispy beef with orange and the more subtly flavoured duck smoked over camphor wood and tea leaves.

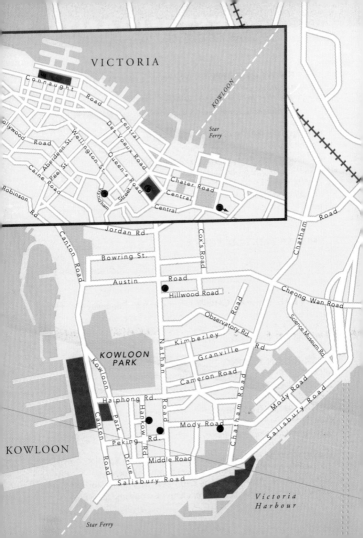

VICTORIA

Connaught   Road

Hollywood

Road

Caine Road

Robinson

Rd.

Aberdeen St.

Wellington St.

Des Voeux Road

Peel St.

Central

Queen's Road

Wyndham St.

Street

Queen's Road

Central

Central

Chater Road

Star Ferry

KOWLOON

Road

Jordan Rd.

Bowring St.

Austin   Road

Cox's Road

Hillwood Road

Observatory Rd.

Cheong Wan Road

Science Museum Rd.

Canton   Road

Kimberley

Nathan

Granville   Rd.

KOWLOON PARK

Cameron Road

Kowloon

Park

Haiphong Rd.

Hankow

Road

Mody Road

Chatham

Road

Mody Road

Salisbury Road

Canton

Road

Peking

Road

Drive

Middle Road

Salisbury   Road

KOWLOON

Chatham   Road

Star Ferry

Victoria
Harbour

Asian

1.ASHOKA G/F 57-59 Wyndham St, Central, HK, tel: 5-255719.
MTR to Central. ❑ Moderate.
A little cramped, but still elegant and popular. Offers a complete range of northern Indian curries and tandoori dishes.

2.SURYA G/F 34-48 Mody Rd, Tsim Sha Tsui, Kowloon, tel: 3-669902.
MTR to Tsim Sha Tsui. ❑ Moderate.
Delicious Indian food and an intimate atmosphere make this a favourite restaurant of the local Indian community.

3.CINTA B/F, New World Harbour View Hotel, 6 Fenwick St, Wan Chai, HK, tel: 5-271199. MTR to Wan Chai; tram.
❑ Inexpensive-moderate.
Indonesian/Malay cuisine – try the sizzling satay which is served on a miniature brazier. Live music.

4.SAWADEE THAI G/F 1 Hillwood Rd, Tsim Sha Tsui, Kowloon, tel: 3-7225577. MTR to Jordan. ❑ Moderate.
The authentic Thai cuisine includes dishes such as tom yam kung *(hot and sour prawn soup with mushrooms) and chicken in green curry sauce.*

5.ARIRANG KOREAN 8-12 Lower Arcade, Hyatt Regency Hotel, Nathan Rd, Kowloon, tel: 3-665551.
MTR to Tsim Sha Tsui. ❑ Moderate.
Mouthwatering barbecued pork, beef, mutton, chicken and prawn dishes with the Korean side dish of kimchi (pickled cabbage and white radish).

6.BENKAY The Landmark, Central, HK, tel: 5-213344.
MTR to Central; Star Ferry. ❑ Expensive.
Stylish Japanese restaurant serving beautifully-presented meals, including sushi, sashimi and teppanyaki.

7.JAVA RIJSTAFFEL 38 Hankow Rd, Tsim Sha Tsui, Kowloon, tel: 3-671230. MTR Tsim Sha Tsui. ❑ Inexpensive.
Tiny Indonesian restaurant. Tasty satay, green curries and gado-gado *(spicy bean-curd salad with peanut sauce).*

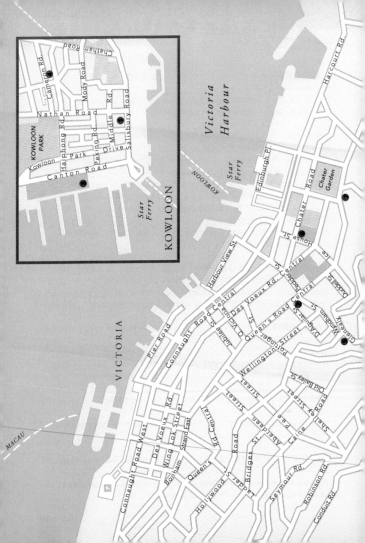

Western

1.GADDI'S The Peninsula Hotel, Salisbury Rd, Tsim Sha Tsui, Kowloon, tel: 3-666251, ext. 3989.
Star Ferry; MTR Tsim Sha Tsui. ❏ Very expensive.
Hong Kong's top dining spot is plush and elegant: French haute cuisine, black tie – and prices to match.

2.JIMMY'S KITCHEN South China Bldg, 1 Wyndham St, Central, HK, tel: 5-265293. MTR Central; tram. ❏ Moderate.
Old-fashioned and popular, with a mixed European and Asian menu, this restaurant first opened its doors over 60 years ago.

3.SAN FRANCISCO STEAKHOUSE 101 Barnton Court, Harbour City, 9 Canton Rd, Tsim Sha Tsui, Kowloon, tel: 3-7227576. MTR Tsim Sha Tsui; Star Ferry. ❏ Moderate-expensive.
Traditional American steakhouse serving tender Angus steaks, burgers, Boston clam chowder, pasta dishes, salads, etc.

4.VALENTINO 60 Cameron Rd, Tsim Sha Tsui, Kowloon, tel: 3-7216449. MTR Tsim Sha Tsui. ❏ Moderate-expensive.
Cosy and romantic atmosphere combined with hearty Italian cooking.

5.MOZART STUB'N G/F 8 Glenealy, Central, HK, tel: 5-221763. ❏ Mon.-Sat. MTR Central. ❏ Moderate-expensive.
A strong European ambience and an Austrian-continental menu including staples like Wiener schnitzel, Hungarian goulash and apfelstrudel.

6.PRINCE'S TAVERN Mezzanine, Prince's Bldg, Chater Rd, Central, HK, tel: 5-239352.
❏ Mon.-Sat. MTR Central; Star Ferry; tram. ❏ Moderate.
Bar-restaurant serving tasty Creole/Cajun food – gumbo, jambalaya, blackened fish, pecan pie, etc.

7.CAT STREET CAFÉ Hilton Hotel, 2 Queen's Rd, Central, HK, tel: 5-233111. MTR Central; Star Ferry; tram. ❏ Moderate.
Pleasant place for lunch (offers a range of Asian and European dishes) or coffee and cakes between bouts of shopping.

1.**LANE CRAWFORD** Lane Crawford House, 70 Queen's Rd, Central, HK. MTR to Central; tram.
Prestigious department store – stylish, up-market and expensive.

2.**MATSUZAKAYA** 2-20 Paterson St, Causeway Bay, HK. MTR to Causeway Bay; tram.
Big, popular Japanese store selling competitively-priced fashions, accessories, shoes and electrical goods.

3.**WING ON** 26 & 211 Des Voeux Rd, Central, HK. MTR to Central, MTR Sheung Wan.
One of Hong Kong's oldest chains, carrying a wide range of bargains including Western imports.

4.**DAIMARU** Kingston & Paterson Sts, Causeway Bay, HK. MTR to Causeway Bay; tram.
Two branches of a Japanese store, the first specializing in household goods, the second in designer fashions, casual wear and accessories.

5.**CHINA PRODUCTS** 19-31 Yee Wo St, Causeway Bay, HK. MTR to Causeway Bay.
A huge selection of low-priced goods from the People's Republic.

6.**CHUNG KIU CHINESE PRODUCTS EMPORIUM** 17 Hankow Rd, Tsim Sha Tsui, Kowloon. MTR to Tsim Sha Tsui; Star Ferry.
Mass-produced arts and crafts. Good for fabrics, quilts, silk items and embroidery.

7.**YUE HWA CHINESE PRODUCTS EMPORIUM** 301-309 Nathan Rd, Tsim Sha Tsui, Kowloon. MTR to Tsim Sha Tsui.
More Chinese bargains, everything from tea sets to do-it-yourself acupuncture kits!

8.**CHINESE ARTS & CRAFTS** Silvercord, 30 Canton Rd, Tsim Sha Tsui, Kowloon. Star Ferry; MTR to Tsim Sha Tsui.
All things Chinese: furniture to furs, carpets to cosmetics, silver to silks.

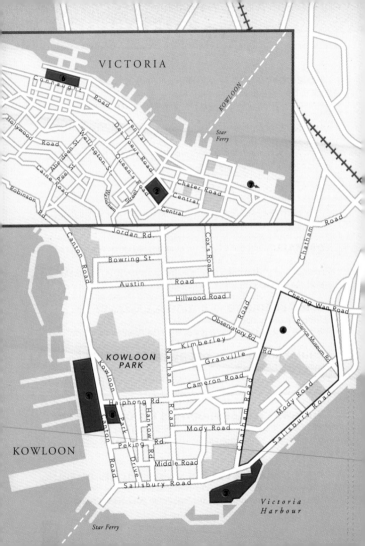

VICTORIA

Connaught Road

Hollywood Road

Wellington St.

Aberdeen St.

Caine Road

Peel St.

Robinson Rd.

Des Voeux Road

Central

Queen's Road

Wyndham St.

Chater Road

Central

Central

KOWLOON

Star Ferry

Jordan Rd.

Bowring St.

Austin

Road

Hillwood Road

Cox's Road

Observatory Rd.

Kimberley

Granville

Cameron Road

Road

Chatham

Road

Cheong Wan Road

Science Museum Rd.

KOWLOON
PARK

Nathan

Road

Kowloon

Park

Haiphong Rd.

Hankow Rd.

Mody Road

Rd

Mody Road

Salisbury Road

Canton Road

Peking Rd.

Dive

Middle Road

Salisbury Road

Chatham Road

Star Ferry

Victoria
Harbour

Canton Road

1.HARBOUR CITY Canton Rd, Tsim Sha Tsui, Kowloon.
Star Ferry; MTR to Tsim Sha Tsui.
Asia's largest shopping centre contains hundreds of mostly up-market shops selling fashion, accessories, jewellery, watches, etc. There are over 40 restaurants too!

2.THE LANDMARK Des Voeux Rd, Central, HK.
MTR to Central; Star Ferry; tram.
Hong Kong's most fashionable centre is an extravaganza of fountains, chrome, glass and escalators, boutiques and art galleries.

3.NEW WORLD CENTRE Salisbury Rd, Tsim Sha Tsui, Kowloon.
Star Ferry; MTR to Tsim Sha Tsui.
Four floors of fashion, leather, hi-fis and jewellery overlooking the harbour, plus a Japanese department store called Tokyu.

4.TSIM SHA TSUI EAST Chatham & Salisbury Rds Kowloon.
Star Ferry, then minibus.
This new district, built on reclaimed land, has 15 shopping centres and countless restaurants.

5.ASIA COMPUTER PLAZA Lower G/F, Silvercord, Canton Rd, Tsim Sha Tsui, Kowloon. Star Ferry; MTR to Tsim Sha Tsui.
Two floors (40,000 sq ft) devoted entirely to computers, peripherals, software, etc.

6.SHUN TAK CENTRE Connaught Rd, Sheung Wan, HK.
MTR to Sheung Wan.
*As well as the usual selection of shops and restaurants, there are many information offices and tour agents for trips to Macau (see **EXCURSION 2**, **A-Z**) and China.*

7.CITY PLAZA Tai Koo Shing Rd, Quarry Bay, HK.
MTR to Tai Koo; tram.
Big new centre (over 400 shops!) situated in the eastern suburb. Fashions for all the family, also toyshops, skating rinks and a bowling alley.

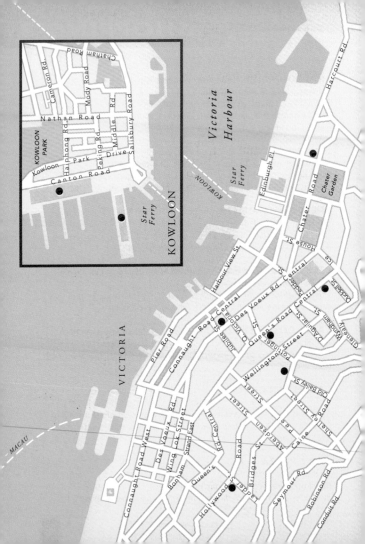

1.**TAI PING CARPETS** G/F Hutchinson House, 10 Harcourt Rd, Central, HK. MTR to Admiralty.
Top quality, locally made, pure-wool carpets. Give sufficient notice and you can even have your own designs custom made.

2.**YUE PO CHAI CURIOS** 132 Hollywood Rd, Sheung Wan, HK. MTR to Sheung Wan; tram.
Crammed with antiques, porcelain, jade, jewellery, ivory, etc.

3.**THE BANYAN TREE** 304 & 311 Ocean Galleries, 3/F, Harbour City, Canton Rd, Tsim Sha Tsui, Kowloon.
Star Ferry; MTR to Tsim Sha Tsui.
Old and new Asian-style furnishings, rattan ware, handicrafts and curios.

4.**THE PEARL GALLERY** 1/F, New World Tower, 16-18 Queen's Rd, Central, HK. MTR to Central; tram.
Jeweller specializing in pearls: cultured, South Seas and distinctively-shaped freshwater varieties.

5.**HELENE BENNETT** 7 Hollywood Rd, Central, HK.
Bus 26 from Statue Square.
Chinese antiques, porcelain, ivory, embroidery, paintings, and more.

6.**MOUNTAIN FOLKCRAFT** 3/F, Ocean Terminal, Tsim Sha Tsui, Kowloon. Star Ferry; MTR to Tsim Sha Tsui.
Fascinating range of crafts, including screen paintings, engravings, and decorative lanterns.

7.**KING FOOK GOLD & JEWELLERY** 30-32 Des Voeux Rd, Central, HK. MTR to Central; tram.
Exquisite gold necklaces and bracelets. Diamonds and other precious stones are sold set, unset, and set to order.

8.**JADE CREATIONS** 410 Lane Crawford House, 70 Queen's Rd, Central, HK. MTR to Central; tram.
Jade in all shades, shapes and sizes – jewellery, figurines, bowls, etc.

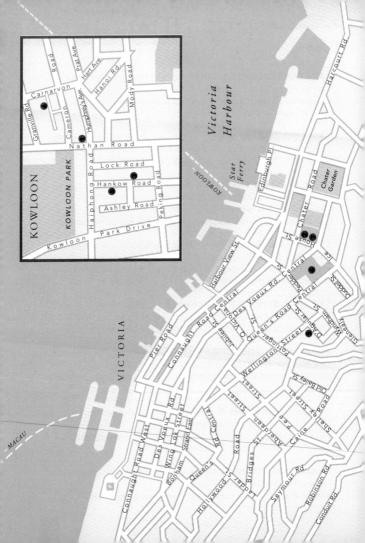

1.**BEL HOMME** 804 Manson House, 74-8 Nathan Rd, Tsim Sha Tsui, Kowloon. MTR to Tsim Sha Tsui.
Dependable, good-quality tailor's shop. Custom-made suits and shirts for both men and women.

2.**WILLIAM'S PHOTO SUPPLY** 138B Prince's Bldg, Chater Rd, Central, HK. MTR to Central; tram; Star Ferry.
Reliable dealer in photographic equipment, binoculars, telescopes, etc.

3.**SWINDON'S** 13-15 Lock Rd, Tsim Sha Tsui, Kowloon.
MTR to Tsim Sha Tsui.
One of the colony's best English-language bookshops. The gratifyingly wide selection includes cheap second-hand books.

4.**THE OPTICAL SHOP** G/F The Landmark, Des Voeux Rd, Central, HK. MTR to Central; tram.
Eyewear and contact lenses are real bargains in Hong Kong so bring your prescription from home. There are branches all over the city.

5.**GREAT WALL LEATHER GOODS** 18 D'Aguilar St, Central, HK.
MTR to Central; tram.
Good-value bags, wallets, belts, briefcases, jackets, coats and suitcases.

6.**TOM LEE MUSIC** 1-9 Cameron Lane, Tsim Sha Tsui, Kowloon.
MTR to Tsim Sha Tsui.
A vast range of acoustic and electronic musical instruments, amplifiers, and audio and hi-fi equipment.

7.**FOOK MING TONG TEA SHOP** 211 Prince's Bldg, Chater Rd, Central, HK. MTR to Central; tram; Star Ferry.
A good selection of Chinese teas and a range of beautifully decorated caddies and tea sets.

8.**WORLD TOP SPORTS GOODS** 49 Hankow Rd, Tsim Sha Tsui, Kowloon. MTR to Tsim Sha Tsui.
All your sporting requirements – both clothing and equipment.

1.GOLF
The Royal Hong Kong Golf Club has three 18-hole courses at Fanling in the New Territories, tel: 0-901211 (Mon.-Fri.; HK$800), and one nine-hole course at Deep Water Bay, tel: 5-8127070 (Mon.-Fri.; HK$200).

2.TENNIS
There are public courts at Victoria Park, Causeway Bay, tel: 5-706186 (see PARKS & GARDENS); Bowen Rd, Wan Chai, tel: 5-282983; and at the HK Tennis Centre, Wong Nei Chong Gap Rd, Happy Valley, tel: 5-749122 (HK$20-40 per hour; try to book in advance).

3.SWIMMING
Hong Kong has numerous beaches, but many are suffering from pollu-tion. The most popular is at Repulse Bay (see CHILDREN, A-Z) where there are lifeguards, showers and changing facilities. Public swimming pools are very popular, especially in summer. You can try Victoria Park Swimming Pool, Hing Fat St, Causeway Bay, or Water World (see CHIL-DREN), a fun park with a variety of pools.

4.WINDSURFING
Sailboards can be hired at most beach resorts, or at Windsurf Boutique, Shop 19-25 Rise Comm. Bldg, 5-11 Granville Circuit, Tsim Sha Tsui, Kowloon, tel: 3-669911 (around HK$40 per hour).

5.WALKING
Hong Kong has 21 country parks with lovely mountain scenery and marked walking trails. Maps and detailed information leaflets are avail-able from Hong Kong Government Publications, GPO Bldg (ground floor), Connaught Pl., Central, HK.

6.JOGGING
There are running courses, complete with exercise stations, in Victoria Park, Causeway Bay (see PARKS & GARDENS), in Kowloon Park, Tsim Sha Tsui (see PARKS & GARDENS), and, best of all, along Bowen Road between Wan Chai and Central (see CITY DISTRICTS) where there are spectacular views of the city and harbour.

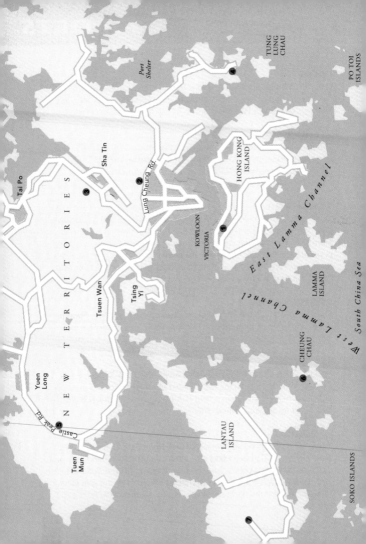

1.MAN MO 126 Hollywood Rd, Sheung Wan, HK.
❏ 0700-1700. Bus 26; MTR Sheung Wan; tram.
Built in the 1840s and dedicated to two deities (see **WALK 2**, **A-Z**).

2.WONG TAI SIN Lung Cheung Rd, Wong Tai Sin, Kowloon.
❏ 0700-1700. MTR Wong Tai Sin.
Rebuilt in the 1970s, on the site of a 1921 temple, and dedicated to the god of healing. The area is crowded with fortune-tellers' stalls. (See **A-Z***)*

3.MAN FAT SZE (TEMPLE OF 10,000 BUDDHAS) Tai Po
Rd, Sha Tin, New Terr.
❏ 0730-1830. MTR Kowloon Tong, then KCR Sha Tin.
This temple is famed for its 12,800 black and gold Buddha images (see **MUSTS**, **A-Z***).*

4.TIN HAU (GREEN TEMPLE) Joss House Bay,
Fat Tong Mun, New Terr.
❏ 0600-1800. MTR Choi Hung, then bus 91.
Site of a spectacular celebration on the birthday of Tin Hau (see **Events***)*

5.CHING CHUNG KOON Castle Peak Rd, Kei Lun Wai, New Terr.
❏ 0600-1800. MTR Tsuen Wan, then bus 66M.
Taoist temple, built in 1949, housing many ancient Chinese treasures, including nearly 4000 books covering 400 years of Taoist history.

6.PAK TAI (TEMPLE OF THE JADE VACUITY)
Cheung Chau Island.
❏ 0600-1800. Ferry.
Dedicated to the 'spirit of the north' protector of fishermen, this temple is the focal point of the Cheung Chau Bun Festival (see **Events***).*

7.PO LIN (PRECIOUS LOTUS) MONASTERY Ngong Ping,
Lantau Peak, Lantau Island.
❏ 24 hr. Ferry, then bus.
This Buddhist monastery is towered over by a 23 m-high, 250-tonne bronze figure of a seated Buddha – one of the world's largest. See **A-Z***.*

The Peak

1-2 hr.

Take a shuttle bus from the Star Ferry and then the Peak Tram (see **Buses, Ferries, Peak Tram**) and begin your walk at Victoria Gap.

The oval-shaped Peak Tower (1) was built 15 years ago and, on the tram terminus level, you will find souvenir shops, a small supermarket, a post office, a bank, an information desk and a viewing balcony with coin-operated telescopes. A lift will take you to the Peak Coffee Shop, the Peak Restaurant and the rooftop viewing terrace. Across the road from the exit onto Peak Road is the Peak Café (2), a charming old Chinese coffee shop set in a former rickshaw station (at the time of writing this was closed down and billed for possible redevelopment as a European-style restaurant). Immediately to the right is a junction of three narrow roads. Climb steeply up the middle one, Mount Austin Road, passing houses and apartments owned by Hong Kong's wealthier residents. At the point where a side road drops down on the right, you can enjoy a magnificent view over the skyscrapers of Central (see **CITY DISTRICTS**) and across the bustling harbour to Kowloon. Continue uphill and after 15 to 25 minutes you will come to the lawns and flower beds of Victoria Peak Garden (3) (see **PARKS & GARDENS**), a popular weekend picnic spot. This was originally the garden of Mountain Lodge, built as the governor's summer residence in 1900. The house was neglected and fell into disrepair following the building of a new retreat at Fanling in 1934, and was finally demolished in 1946. At the far side of the garden is a wide platform with a viewing indicator, which offers expansive views to the west over Lantau Island and, on a clear day, across to Macau (see **EXCURSION 2**, **A-Z**).

The very summit of The Peak is occupied by a wireless station and is not open to the public, so return to the garden and take the lower of the two footpaths that cut across the side of the smaller hill on the right, leading towards a bridge over a little creek. Don't cross the bridge, but keep to the path that curves round to the right as it follows the contours of the far side of the hill. It is known as Governor's Walk and it leads down to Lugard Road. Turn right and follow this pleasant, leafy path all the way back to Peak Tower. Try to time your walk to arrive at the northernmost part of Lugard Road around sunset when you will be treated to the most spectacular panorama of the Mid Levels and

Western District (see **CITY DISTRICTS**), and the thousand twinkling lights of ships in the anchorage off Stonecutters Island. The final stretch of path offers glimpses down to the bright lights of Central and Kowloon. End your walk with a well-earned meal at one of the restaurants in the Peak Tower before taking the Peak Tram back to Central.

See **CITY DISTRICTS**, **MUSTS**.

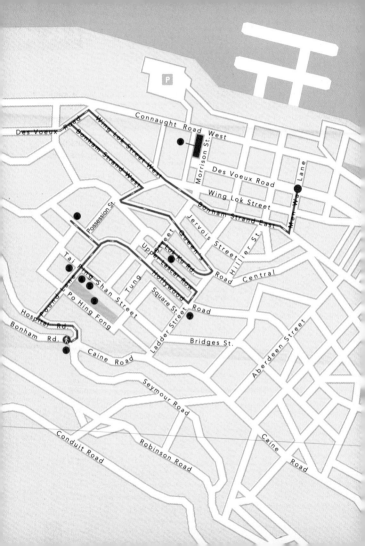

2-4 hr.

Take a taxi or bus 3 from Jardine House, Connaught Road (see **Buses, Taxis**) and begin your walk at Hop Yat Church (1), 2 Bonham Road. The church, in neo-Gothic style, was built in 1925 by Hong Kong's earliest Chinese Christian congregation. Cross the road and turn left into Hospital Road, then go right down the steps of Pound Lane, passing Blake Garden (2) on the right, to Tai Ping Shan Street. This is one of the oldest parts of the city and was one of the first 'Chinatown' areas during the early days of British occupation.

On the left-hand corner of Pound Lane and Tai Ping Shan Street is Pak Shing Temple (3) dating from 1851, but rebuilt in 1895 when the area was cleared following an outbreak of plague. It was originally built by local people to house the ancestral tablets of relatives who died away from their home villages, and as a holding chamber for the dead await-

ing shipment back to mainland China. Climb the stairs and take a look inside. The temple houses over 3000 ancestral tablets (rectangular pieces of wood carved with the name and birth date of the deceased). The red, painted altar bears a statue of Dei Zhong Wang, the god associated with ancestor worship. On the right-hand corner, up the steps from Pound Lane, stands Sui Tsing Paak Temple (4). From the verandah, with its smoking incense coils, go left into the Main Hall where you will find the altar with its glass case containing a statue of Sui Tsing Paak ('The Pacifying General'). He is believed to have the power to cure sickness, and was brought here from China in 1894 in the hope that he would cure the plague that was then devastating the area. You will also see the rows of Tai Sui (Sixty Gods) images, one for each of the sixty years in the cycle of the Chinese calendar. Seeking good fortune, local people make offerings to the god representing their year of birth. Next door, and a little further up the hill, is Kuan Yin Temple (5), dedicated to the Goddess of Mercy. The image of the goddess, who is popular with women praying for strong sons and beautiful daughters, is believed to have been carved, in 1840, from a piece of wood found in the sea by the wife of one of the temple's founders.

Return to Pound Lane and descend to Hollywood Road. You will find

Possession Street a short distance to the left. This street marks the spot where Captain Charles Elliot first hoisted the Union Jack, on 26 January, 1841, to claim the colony for Britain. (This area once constituted the waterfront, before land reclamation extended into the harbour.) A little further along are workshops (6) producing distinctive Chinese coffins with concave wooden sides and lids. Retrace your steps and browse among the many fascinating shops, selling Asian antiques, curios and furniture, that line this stretch of Hollywood Road. At the junction with Ladder Street stands the fine old Man Mo Temple (7) (see **TEMPLES, A-Z**), and you will see a traditional, red, British-style letter box right on the corner. Ladder Street is so named because it consists entirely of steps. It was originally built to allow the passage of sedan chairs ferrying wealthy residents from the town to their homes in the Mid Levels (see **A-Z**).

After visiting the temple, go down Ladder Street and left along Upper Lascar Row, better known as Cat Street, a lane packed with pavement vendors selling all kinds of junk and bric-a-brac (see **MARKETS**). Turn right at Tung Street and right again along Lok Ku Road. If you like, look in at the Cat Street Galleries (8), an interesting collection of shops dealing in antiques, carpets, ceramics, furniture, jade, lacquer ware and much more. Continue down to Queen's Road Central. Go left, passing more shops selling assorted household goods, then turn right and then left into Bonham Strand West.

This is the heart of the old Chinese commercial area of Nam Pak Hong. The streets here are lined with the premises of wholesale dealers in all kinds of exotic goods – medicinal herbs, leaves, seeds, flowers, roots, crushed pearls, rhino horn, deer antlers, tigers' paws and more. The roots you see in the glass preserving jars in the shop windows are highly-prized ginseng roots. When you reach Des Voeux Road (with the tram lines) wander along to the left for a bit to see (and smell!) the shops selling dried seafood – heaps of orange shrimps, strings of fish, flattened squid and shelves of pale-yellow sharks' fins. If you feel tired at this point, then catch a tram back to Central (see **CITY DISTRICTS**), otherwise retrace your steps and turn right into Wing Lok Street West, where there are more interesting shops, walk past Morrison Street which leads to the busy Western Market (9) and continue into Bonham Strand East.

Here, and in the neighbouring streets of Jervois and Hillier, you will find gold dealers, shops selling rattan ware and, in season (Oct.-Feb.), Hong Kong's notorious snake shops. The Chinese believe that snakes give you strength and potency; and visitors are either fascinated or horrified by the snake soup, cocktails of snake blood and brandy, and green snake wine made from the snake bile.

End your walk with a stroll down Man Wa Lane on the left. A line of little stalls houses the workshops of craftsmen who carve traditional seals, or 'chops'. These have been used by the Chinese for over 3000 years to mark documents and works of art with a personal 'signature'. They are fashioned from a variety of materials including wood, stone, porcelain, ivory and jade. You can have one made with your name rendered into Chinese characters – it takes about an hour, but you can wander off and collect it later if you don't want to stay and watch it being made.

At the intersection of Man Wa Lane and Des Voeux Road you have the choice of taking either a tram (see **A-Z**) or the MTR (see **A-Z**) back to Central (see **CITY DISTRICTS**).

71

Victoria Harbour

Hung Hing Road

Fleming Road

Marsh Road

Gloucester Road

Yee Wo St

Hennessy Road

Rd.

Wan Chai Rd.

Johnston Rd.

Leighton Road

Queen's Road

Nullah Lane

Wan Chai

Wong Nai Chung Road

East

Kennedy Rd.

Bowen Road

Wan Chai Gap Rd.

Wong Nai

Chung Road

Stubbs Rd.

Stubbs Road

Bowen Road

Stubbs Rd.

Stubbs Rd.

Black's Link

Middle Gap Rd.

439

MOUNT
CAMERON

Bowen Road to Wan Chai

1-2 hr.

Take bus 15 (see **Buses**) from the Star Ferry terminal and begin your walk at the bus stop beside Longland Apartments (1), 41 Stubbs Road, above Happy Valley.

From the bus stop, cross the road, head back downhill, and descend a flight of steps on the left to reach Bowen Road. Walk left along the narrow road (really only a footpath since there is no traffic) for about 200 m until you see some steps with a red handrail leading up to the left. Follow the stairs up, and then left, to reach the Earth God Shrine (2), set against a rock face under a red corrugated iron roof. Earth gods have their origins in ancient animistic beliefs and have been worshipped by the Chinese for thousands of years. They are neighbourhood spirits that protect and oversee the affairs of the local community. The shrine is decorated with plastic windmills and bits of ribbon, and there are earth-filled trays for holding joss sticks.

Go back down the steps and continue along Bowen Road. All along the path you will see little shrines in the rocks and joss sticks poking up from the verge. A short distance from the foot of the steps is a bridge spanning a stream. From here you will get a good view over Happy Valley (see **A-Z**), dominated by the Royal Hong Kong Jockey Club's racecourse (3) (see **Sports**). Horse racing in the colony is thought to have originated with the military in the mid-1840s, and is immensely popular today. The Hong Kong Cemetery (4), lying to the west of the racecourse, dates from 1845, and is actually five cemeteries in one (north to south these are the Muslim, Roman Catholic, Colonial, Parsee and Hindu cemeteries). If your walk coincides with the sixth, 16th or 26th day of the lunar month, the next stretch of path will be crowded with local people and fortune-tellers, and lined with stalls selling incense; for on these days unmarried girls, forlorn lovers, wives and widows all come to make offerings at Yan Yuen Shek (5) (Lovers' Rock, also called Amah Rock) and pray for an ideal husband or a reunion with a loved one. Climb up the steep stairway between boulders decorated with shrines to reach the 9 m-high granite pinnacle with its terrific view of Wan Chai (see **CITY DISTRICTS**) and the harbour. Descend and continue along Bowen Road until you reach Wan Chai Gap Road, and then turn sharp right heading downhill. Alternatively, continue all the

way along Bowen Road to get to the Peak Tram (see **WALK 1, A-Z**) above
Central (see **CITY DISTRICTS**).

At the foot of Wan Chai Gap Road go right along Kennedy Road for a
short distance, then turn left down the steps at the top of Stone Nullah
Lane and visit the Pak Tai Temple (6) on the right. This temple dates
from 1863, and houses a three metre-high copper statue of Pak Tai
(spirit of the north, protector of fishermen, and restorer of harmony).
Note the Tai Sui (Sixty Gods – see **WALK 2**) on the left-hand wall.
Leaving the temple, go down Stone Nullah Lane, cross Queen's Road
East and go into Wan Chai Road. Finish your walk with a leisurely stroll
around the street market here, which is packed with colourful fruit and
vegetable stalls, butchers' stalls hung with their traditional red lights,
and stalls selling cheap jeans and shirts. To return to Central, follow
Wan Chai Road or Tai Wo Street to the tram lines on Johnston Road, or
continue on for a further block to reach Hennessy Road and Wan Chai
MTR (see **A-Z**) station.

Aberdeen: This town on the south side of Hong Kong Island is named after Lord Aberdeen, British Foreign Secretary in the 1840s, and is one of the colony's oldest settlements. Its original Chinese name was Heung Kong (Fragrant Harbour), supposedly recalling a local incense factory, and is said to have given its name to the whole island. Today, the Chinese population still calls the town Heung Kong Tsai, or Little Hong Kong. The harbour here is jammed with hundreds of junks and sampans and is famous for its numerous boat yards. Sampan women will clamour for your attention, offering trips round the harbour or out to one of the three garishly decorated floating restaurants (see **Eating Out**) in Shum Wan harbour to the east (such as the Jumbo Floating Restaurant). The town itself has a number of interesting shops and a Tin Hau Temple dating from 1851. The HKTA (see **Tourist Information**) issues an interesting fact sheet on Aberdeen.

Accidents & Breakdowns: If you are involved in a road accident, exchange insurance details and, if anyone has been hurt, call an ambulance and the police. In the event of a breakdown, telephone your car rental company and they will arrange to pick you up and replace the vehicle. See **Consulates**, **Driving**, **Emergency Numbers**.

Accommodation: Hong Kong has no shortage of first-class hotels. Unfortunately for the budget-conscious traveller, these are mostly deluxe establishments and there is very little in the way of low-cost accommodation. There is no official rating system in the colony, but the HKTA (see **Tourist Information**) publishes a hotel guide listing approved hotels, along with their facilities and prices. Most hotels are concentrated in Tsim Sha Tsui, Central and Causeway Bay (see CITY DISTRICTS).
There is no particular high or low season as Hong Kong's hotels tend to be busy all year round, so you are advised to book well in advance. However, there is a Hong Kong Hotels Association desk at Kai Tak Airport (see **Airport**) where help is given in finding rooms for those who do arrive without a booking (tel: 3-838380).
You can expect to pay around HK$500-1000 for a twin room in most of of Hong Kong's hotels, but this rises to about HK$1000-1500 in the

deluxe hotels. A 10% service charge and 5% government tax will be added to your bill. Cheap rooms and backpackers' hostels are concentrated in and around the crumbling, high-rise Chungking Mansions on Nathan Road, Tsim Sha Tsui, where prices range from HK$40-50 for a dormitory bed to HK$150-250 for a basic, air-conditioned room. There is also a YMCA at 23 Waterloo Rd, Yau Ma Tei, Kowloon, tel: 3-7719111, and at Salisbury Rd, Tsim Sha Tsui, Kowloon, tel: 3-692211; and the YWCA is at 5 Man Fuk Rd, Waterloo Hill, Kowloon, tel: 3-7139211. See **Youth Hostels**.

Airport: Kai Tak International Airport, 5 km east of central Kowloon, is a modern and efficient airport: facilities include banks, bureaux de change, a hotel bookings desk, HKTA (see **Tourist Information**) and MTIB (Macau Tourist Information Board) information desks, free telephones, a left-luggage office, a post-office and shops.
After going through customs, go straight onto one of the hotel buses or tour coaches, or turn towards the Arrival Hall for public transport into the city. The Airbus service departs every 15 min (0700-2300): bus A1 goes to the Tsim Sha Tsui hotel area (HK$5), bus A2 to Central (HK$8), and bus A3 to Causeway Bay (HK$8). See **CITY DISTRICTS**.

Taxis to the same areas cost around HK$25-30, HK$45-50, and HK$50-60 respectively, and journey times are around 15 min to Kowloon and 25-30 min to Hong Kong Island.

Leaving from the airport, you are required to pay a departure tax of HK$100 (HK$60 for children aged 2-11).

Phone 3-7697531 for airport and flight information.

Aw Boon Haw (Tiger Balm) Gardens: See CHILDREN, PARKS & GARDENS.

Baby-sitters: Most hotels can provide a baby-sitting service. See CHILDREN.

Bank of China Building: This striking new skyscraper, designed

by the Chinese-American architect I. M. Pei (who also designed the controversial glass pyramid at the Louvre in Paris), looms portentously over the nearby Legislative Council Building (see **A-Z**). Its 305 m-high, 70-storey tower dominates Hong Kong's Central district (see **CITY DISTRICTS**).

Banks: See **Currency, Money, Opening Times**.

Best Buys: Hong Kong has to be the ultimate shoppers' paradise: you can buy almost anything here, and usually at lower prices than anywhere else in the world. Certain goods like cameras and computers are not the bargains they once were and it pays to check the prices at home for equivalent goods before making a big purchase here. Asian arts, crafts and antiques are some of the most popular purchases, especially carpets and ceramics. Antique stores abound along Hollywood Road in Central and Western (see **CITY DISTRICTS**), and a fascinating range of Chinese products can be found in any of the Chinese emporiums (see **SHOPPING 1**). Gold jewellery, diamonds and pearls are not subject to tax and therefore make a particularly good buy. Jade jewellery and other jade articles are widely available in a range of qualities and prices. Attractive teak, rosewood and rattan furniture is also popular, with shops and manufacturers concentrated in the Wan Chai area (see **CITY DISTRICTS**). Electrical and electronic equipment is sold in countless shops crammed into the backstreets of Kowloon (video cameras and recorders are a particularly good buy here). For a very reason-

able price one of Hong Kong's many tailors can run up a couple of custom-made suits during your stay, but be sure to stick to HKTA-approved (see **Tourist Information**) businesses if you don't want your suit to unravel before you get home! Leather goods are also attractively priced. Lastly, eyewear and contact lenses constitute an excellent bargain which is often overlooked. See **MARKETS**, **SHOPPING**, **Shopping**.

Bicycle Hire: Hong Kong's hills and congested traffic make cycling a bad bet. However, bicycles can be hired to tour the more peaceful roads of Lantau Island (see **Outlying Islands**). They are available from the Silvermine Beach Hotel, Silvermine Bay, for around HK$25 per day.

Budget:	Hotel breakfast	HK$50-70
	Lunch	HK$50-150
	Dim sum	HK$5 (per dish)
	Dinner	HK$100-250
	Cinema ticket	HK$25
	Museum ticket	usually free
	Afternoon tea	HK$50
	Coffee	HK$3-4

House wine	from HK$50 (carafe)
Beer	HK$13-25 (pint)
MTR ticket	HK$2.50-6.00

Buses: A good double-decker bus service covers Hong Kong Island, Kowloon and the New Territories, but buses can get very crowded during rush hours and they are not air-conditioned. The two main bus companies are the blue-and-white liveried CMB (China Motor Bus), largely serving Hong Kong Island, and the red-and-cream KMB (Kowloon Motor Bus), mostly serving Kowloon and the New Territories. Buses run every 10-20 min (0600-2400) and fares range from HK$1-7. The exact fare is required and must be dropped into the box by the driver (no ticket is issued). The Central Bus Terminal is at Exchange Square, Connaught Rd, Central, and a bus guide detailing routes, times and fares is available from CMB Head Office, 510 King's Rd, North Point, Hong Kong. Tel: 5-658556 (CMB) or 3-7454466 (KMB) for detailed information on services. The HKTA (see **Tourist Information**) also issues leaflets giving full details of most bus routes.

The red and yellow, 14-seater minibuses you will see on Hong Kong streets are used mainly by local people, however their destinations are written on the front in English as well as Chinese (in tiny letters above the Chinese). They can be hailed like taxis and they will set you down anywhere stopping is allowed (not at CMB and KMB bus stops). To stop a minibus, shout *yau lok*. Pay the driver as you exit (generally HK$2-6), no change is given.

Maxicabs are like minibuses, but have a green stripe instead of a red one. They run on fixed routes and cannot be hailed just anywhere. Fares are HK$1-4 and you pay when you board. The most useful service is No. 1 which runs every 5 min from the Kowloon Star Ferry terminal to Tsim Sha Tsui East (HK$1). See **Airport**, **Transport**.

Cameras & Photography: Stores selling film and photographic equipment, often at bargain prices, can be found in almost every shopping centre and in every street in Tsim Sha Tsui (see CITY DISTRICTS). Film, especially, is a good buy at around two-thirds of the UK price. Apart from Kodachrome, which must be sent to Australia, processing is fast and also inexpensive. One drawback is Hong Kong's hot and humid climate which can be detrimental to film and cameras, so, if possible, store these in an air-conditioned room or in a refrigerator when you are not using them. Remember that many Chinese people, especially country folk and the elderly, may object to being photo-graphed, therefore show good manners and always ask permission first. It is also wise to ask before taking pictures in temples.

Camping: There are no camp sites convenient to the main urban areas. Camping is permitted at a number of Youth Hostels in the New Territories – contact the YHA office for details (see **Youth Hostels**). There are other independent camp sites on Lantau Island (see **Outlying Islands**) – contact the HKTA for details (see **Tourist Information**).

Car Hire: To hire a car in Hong Kong you must be at least 25 years old and have held a driving licence for a minimum of two years (either a UK licence or an International Driving Permit is acceptable). Credit cards are accepted by all the major rental companies, but cash payments require a deposit and payment in advance. Typical rates (including insurance) are around HK$300-400 per day and HK$2000-2500 per week. Hire firms include Avis, 50 Po Loi St, Hung Hom, Kowloon, tel: 3-346007, and National, Harbour Crystal Centre, Granville Rd, Tsim Sha Tsui East, Kowloon, tel: 3-671047.
Chauffeur-driven cars can also be hired from most hotels for around HK$120 per hour. See **Driving**.

Cat Street: See MARKETS, WALK 2.

Causeway Bay: See CITY DISTRICTS.

Central District: See CITY DISTRICTS.

Cheung Chau: See Outlying Islands.

Chemists: Most pharmacies are open daily 0900-1800, and some city-centre branches stay open until 2000. Try the Watson's chain which has branches all over the city, including Shop 12, 1/F Hilton Hotel Arcade, 2 Queen's Rd, Central, Hong Kong, and 101 Nathan Rd, Tsim Sha Tsui, Kowloon. See **Health**.

Children: See CHILDREN, **Baby-sitters**.

Ching Chung Koon Temple: See TEMPLES.

City Hall: See ENTERTAINMENT.

Clearwater Bay: The Clearwater Bay Golf and Country Club occupies a seaside setting on Sai Kung Peninsula, New Territories, and offers golf, tennis, squash, badminton, swimming and saunas. Contact the HKTA (see **Tourist Information**) for details of day trips to the club.

Climate: Hong Kong, lying just south of the Tropic of Cancer, has a subtropical monsoon climate. Winter (Jan.-Mar.) is cold or cool (13-18°C) and often overcast and wet. Spring (Mar.-May) brings the south-west monsoon and is warmer (18-28°C) and more humid, with wet misty weather broken by increasing sunny spells. Summer (June-Sept.) is the typhoon season: hot (26-31°C), humid and very wet. Approaching typhoons (hurricanes) are announced by graded warnings ranging from one, which is merely cautionary, to ten, which means a direct hit is expected within hours. If a typhoon is expected, return to your hotel and stay indoors until the danger is past. Autumn (Oct.-Dec.) is the best time to visit as it brings pleasantly warm (16-27°C), sunny weather, the humidity is relatively low and the nights are cool.

Complaints: For complaints relating to businesses that are members of the HKTA (see **Tourist Information**) contact the HKTA on 5-244191, ext. 278 (0900-1700 Mon.-Fri., 0900-1300 Sat). You can find out which ones are members by consulting the HKTA's *Official Guide to Shopping and Eating Out*. Complaints about other shops should be addressed to the Consumer Council, 3/F Asian House, 1 Hennessy Rd, Wan Chai, Hong Kong, tel: 5-200511. Complaints about taxi drivers should be reported on the police's Crime Hotline, tel: 5-277177.

Consulates:

Eire – 8/F Prince's Bldg, Chater Rd, Central, Hong Kong, tel: 5-226022.
Australia – 23-24/F Harbour Centre, Harbour Rd, Wan Chai, Hong Kong, tel: 5-731881.
Canada – 12/F Tower 1, Exchange Sq., Connaught Rd, Central, Hong Kong, tel: 5-8104321.
New Zealand – 34/F Jardine House (formerly Connaught Centre), Connaught Rd, Central, Hong Kong, tel: 5-255044.
USA – 26 Garden Rd, Central, Hong Kong, tel: 5-239011.

Conversion Chart:

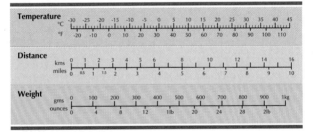

Credit Cards: See **Money**.

Crime & Theft: Hong Kong is a fairly safe place as most large cities go, but it is still sensible to take the usual precautions against theft: leave any valuables in the hotel safe (not in your room) and beware of pickpockets in crowded areas, especially in shopping centres and on public transport. Any theft should be reported immediately to the police. If your passport is lost or stolen, contact your consulate as well as the police. See **Consulates**, **Emergency Numbers**, **Insurance**, **Police**.

Currency: The unit of currency in Hong Kong is the Hong Kong dollar (HK$), which is divided into 100 cents (c). Notes are issued in

denominations of 10, 20, 50, 100, 500 and 1000 HK$. The coins in cir-
culation are worth 10, 20 and 50 cents, and 1, 2 and 5 HK$. There are
no restrictions on the transfer of currency into or out of the colony.
See **Money**.

Customs Allowances:

Duty Free Into:	Cigarettes	or	Cigars	or	Tobacco	Spirits	or	Wine
HONG KONG	200		50		250 g	1 *l*		1 *l*
U.K.	200		50		250 g	1 *l*		2 *l*

Dentists: See **Health**.

Disabled People: Hong Kong, with its steep hills, crowded streets
and multistorey shopping centres, is not an easy city for disabled travellers to negotiate. The MTR (see **A-Z**) has no facilities for the disabled,
however Kai Tak Airport (see **Airport**), the Hong Kong Arts Centre, the
Academy of Performing Arts, the City Hall (see **ENTERTAINMENT**) and
some of the newer shopping centres (e.g. the City Plaza – see **SHOPPING
2**) have provided special ramps and toilets. A useful *Guide For
Physically Handicapped Visitors in Hong Kong* is available from the
HKTA (see **Tourist Information**).

Drinks: Tea, unadulterated by milk or sugar, and often scented with
jasmine or chrysanthemum petals, is the traditional accompaniment to
a Chinese meal. It is served in dainty china cups without handles.
When your teapot requires refilling, simply turn the lid upside down
and the waiter will bring a fresh brew. Coffee and Indian tea are available from any hotel coffee shop, and a wide range of cooling soft

drinks and mineral waters are sold in shops and fast-food outlets. Tap water is safe to drink, but most hotels provide bottled, purified water for drinking.

The most popular alcoholic drinks are beer (Tsing Tao, from China, and San Miguel, brewed locally by a Filipino brewery company) and cognac. European table wines are available but tend to be expensive, so try Chinese rice wine which is similar to Japanese saki.

Driving: Self-drive hire cars are not recommended as a way of getting around the city as the streets are very congested and parking is extremely difficult. It is much easier to use public transport which is efficient and inexpensive. However, a car can be a good way of exploring the New Territories and road surfaces are generally excellent. Drive on the left and give way to traffic on the right at roundabouts. Speed limits are 50 kph in built-up areas and as indicated by road signs elsewhere. The wearing of seat belts is compulsory. Call the Hong Kong Automobile Association (AA) on 5-743394 for details of membership and reciprocal rights with other motoring organizations. See **Accidents & Breakdowns**, **Car Hire**, **Parking**, **Petrol**, **Transport**.

Drugs: It is an offence to carry in, manufacture, import, export, cultivate, possess or consume any form of controlled drug. Penalties for offences are severe.

Eating Out: After shopping, eating is Hong Kong's next greatest attraction, with over 30,000 restaurants offering just about any cuisine you could ask for: French, German, Italian, English, Austrian, Dutch, Caribbean, Creole, American, Mexican, Indian, Indonesian, Malay, Thai, Japanese, Korean, Vietnamese, Filipino – and more. But naturally, the most predominant and popular of the numerous cuisines on offer are the regional Chinese ones (see **Food**).

Chinese restaurants range from street-side *dai pai dongs* (pavement stalls, with little tables and stools, selling basic, inexpensive meals) to *dim sum* (see **Food**) restaurants and tea shops, popular family restaurants, vast seafood emporiums, and the expensive gourmet establishments located in the top hotels (the range in prices is correspondingly

wide). A meal can cost anything from HK$10 at a pavement stall to over HK$500 at a luxury hotel. When dining in a Chinese restaurant, it is usual to order one dish per person, and one more. These are then set out in the centre of the table for everyone to help themselves, and are accompanied by rice and tea. Your place setting will consist of a pair of chopsticks (tourist restaurants will provide a fork if necessary, but try the chopsticks first as it's really not as difficult as it looks), a large bowl for rice, a small bowl for tea, and a porcelain spoon for slurping soup and serving yourself from the main dishes. To eat rice with chopsticks, hold the bowl close to your mouth and shovel it in. Don't worry about spilling food on the tablecloth – everybody does it, even the locals.

Most restaurants are concentrated in Tsim Sha Tsui, Central and Causeway Bay (see **CITY DISTRICTS**). *Dai pai dongs* can be found all over the place and there is a good range of seafood stalls at Temple Street Night Market (see **MARKETS**). As a rule they do not have menus – just point to the dishes you want and they will be served up with rice.

There are three famous floating restaurants at Aberdeen Harbour (see **Aberdeen**) which cater for the tourist trade, but they are very busy and tend to be grossly overpriced. Instead why not go to one of the popular (specially at lunchtimes) dim sum restaurants. Here the waiters wheel around trolleys of dim sum in their little bamboo baskets – again just point out the ones you want. The bill is calculated by counting the number of empty baskets lying on your table at the end of the meal. In contrast, if you find yourself craving for Western-style junk food, you will find fast-food outlets such as Macdonald's and Kentucky Fried Chicken all over the city.

Useful guides to eating out in Hong Kong are the HKTA's (see **Tourist Information**) *Official Guide to Shopping and Eating Out,* which lists approved establishments, and *Hong Kong's 100 Best Restaurants,* which is available from bookshops and costs HK$55.

The pricing categories adopted in the **RESTAURANTS** topic in this book refer to a dinner for one without drinks:

Very Expensive	over HK$500
Expensive	HK$250-500
Moderate	HK$100-250
Inexpensive	less than HK$100

See **RESTAURANTS**, **Food**.

Electricity: 200V/50Hz AC. Three-pin plugs are used and adaptors are required.

Emergency Numbers:

Police, fire and ambulance	999
Queen Mary Hospital	5-8192111

Events: The dates of Chinese festivals are calculated according to the lunar calendar and vary from year to year so check with the HKTA (see **Tourist Information**) for exact dates.

Mid January-mid February: Hong Kong Arts Festival, international theatre, music, dance etc.

Late January-early February: Chinese New Year, family celebrations with banquets, parties, new clothes and flowers, plus a fireworks display over the harbour.

April: Ching Ming Festival, families sweep and tidy their ancestors' graves, and burn paper cars, houses, money etc. thereby sending them to their ancestors in the afterlife; Birthday of Tin Hau, temples dedicated to this Queen of Heaven (the protector of fisherfolk) are the settings for the festivities, and decorated fishing junks, sampans and ferries visit Tin Hau Temple (see **TEMPLES**) in Joss House Bay.

May: Cheung Chau Bun Festival, six days of costumed parades on Cheung Chau Island (see **Outlying Islands**) creates a carnival atmosphere which culminates in the distribution of special buns from huge bun towers to ensure good luck and prosperity. See **TEMPLES**.

May-June: Dragon Boat Festival, originates in the fishermen's commemoration of the Chinese poet-hero, Qu Yuan and is now celebrated by spectacular Dragon Boat races with competing teams coming from all over the world.

August: Festival of the Hungry Ghosts, spirits are freed to roam the earth, incense and paper money is burned, and food is laid out at roadsides to appease the ghosts.
September: Mooncake Festival, lantern-carrying crowds gather in parks and other open spaces (see **PARKS & GARDENS – VICTORIA PARK**) to admire the harvest moon and eat traditional pastry 'mooncakes', inside of which an egg yolk hangs suspended in sweet bean paste to represent the moon.
October: Cheung Yeung Festival, more sweeping of graves and offerings to ancestors, as well as climbs to high places to ensure good fortune (in memory of the legendary man who escaped a natural disaster by following a fortune-teller's advice to seek high ground); Festival of Asian Arts, two weeks of traditional music, song, dance and theatre with groups from all over Asia.
December: spectacular Christmas illuminations in the streets and shops of Central and Tsim Sha Tsui (see **CITY DISTRICTS**).

Exchange Square: This futuristic building on Connaught Road, Central, Hong Kong, with its three graceful towers faced in pink granite and mirrored glass, houses the Hong Kong Stock Exchange. Designed by the Swiss architect Remo Riva, the building boasts a computer-controlled living environment, talking lifts and an attractive atrium with fountains, greenery and changing art exhibitions.

Ferries: The green and white Star Ferries are not only one of Hong Kong's most famous sights, but also provide a vital link between Hong Kong Island and Kowloon. The service has been running since 1898 and there are now ten ferryboats, all named after stars: *Shining Star, Evening Star, Northern Star*, etc. These run every few minutes between Central and Tsim Sha Tsui and take seven minutes to make the crossing

94

(0630-2330; HK$0.60 lower deck, HK$0.80 upper deck; pay at turn-stiles). There are also services from Tsim Sha Tsui to Wan Chai (0730-2300; HK$1.00), and from Central to Hung Hom, terminus of the Kowloon-Canton Railway (0700-1920; HK$0.90).

The Hong Kong & Yau Ma Tei Ferry Co. (HYF) runs ferry services from the Outlying Districts Ferry Pier, Central (west of the Star Ferry terminal) to various piers in Kowloon, and to the outlying islands (see **A-Z**) of Lamma, Lantau, Cheung Chau, Peng Chau and Po Toi.

Hydrofoils and jetfoils make regular crossings to Macau (see **EXCURSION 2, A-Z**) from the Macau Ferry Terminal, Sheung Wan, Hong Kong, and there are regular ship, hydrofoil and hovercraft services to Guangzhou in China (see **EXCURSION 3, A-Z**).

The HKTA (see **Tourist Information**) has a schedule of all ferry services. It can be obtained from the HKTA office at Kowloon Star Ferry terminal, or you can call 3-7225555 or 5-244191 for information.
See **Transport**.

Flagstaff House Museum of Tea Ware: See MUSEUMS.

Food: Hong Kong is unarguably the best place in the world to enjoy Chinese food in any of its regional variations, however since 94% of the population hails from Guangdong (Canton) province, it's no surprise that Cantonese cuisine tops the bill. This is also the style of Chinese cooking that will be most familiar to visitors used to eating in Chinese restaurants in Britain. It is based on ingredients such as fresh vegetables, beef, pork, chicken and seafood, which are flavoured with sesame oil, ginger, spring onions, soy sauce and rice wine, and cooked very quickly at an extremely high temperature (stir-fried or steamed in a wok) to retain the natural flavours. A uniquely Cantonese traditional food is dim sum, a selection of bite-sized hors d'oeuvres composed of steamed, boiled or fried spring rolls, dumplings and pastry parcels containing chopped meat, seafood and vegetables – usually served from 6 am until after lunchtime as a snack or light meal.

Peking, once the home of China's Imperial Court, has a long tradition of gourmet cooking. The most famous dish is Peking Duck, coated in honey and soy sauce before being slowly roasted. The crispy, succulent skin is served with thin pancakes, slivers of cucumber and spring onion, and a sweet plum sauce. This should be followed by the meat, sauteed with bean sprouts, and rounded off with a tasty soup made with the carcass. Beggar's Chicken, made by stuffing a chicken with mushrooms, cabbage, herbs and onions, then wrapping it in lotus leaves and coating it in clay before baking it, is another popular dish. When the cooked bird is brought to the table the guest of honour cracks open the clay casing with a mallet, allowing the mouthwatering aroma to escape.

Shanghai food is richer and heavier than Cantonese, and is especially popular in winter. Traditional dishes include Drunken Chicken, cooked in strong rice wine, eels cooked in wine and garlic, and the seasonal 'hairy crabs' which appear in the restaurants in autumn and are a great favourite.

Hearty Chiu Chow meals always begin and end with a tiny thimbleful of powerful 'Iron Buddha' tea which, it is claimed, contains more caffeine than even the strongest coffee. Menus include dishes such as rich shark's fin and bird's nest soups, sumptuous seafood and chicken dishes, and braised goose with soy sauce served with pieces of

fried goose blood (not as bad as it sounds!).
Szechuan dishes, liberally laced with chillies, peppers and garlic, are notoriously hot and spicy. Not to be missed is smoked duck, Szechuan-style: the duck is marinated in rice wine, ginger, peppercorns, cinnamon and orange peel, then coated in tea leaves and smoked over a fire spiked with camphor wood.
Hong Kong has many Chinese vegetarian restaurants serving delicious meals concocted from mushrooms and other fungi, bean curd, bean sprouts, bamboo shoots, baby corn etc. The more adventurous diner can sample more unusual dishes in Chinese restaurants and in street-side *dai pai dongs*, such as fried intestines or brains, snake soup, bear's paw, duck's feet, frog, turtle, fish eyes, fish lips … and so on. See RESTAURANTS, **Eating Out**.

Food Street: This covered thoroughfare running between Kingston Street and Gloucester Road in Causeway Bay (see CITY DISTRICTS) is lined with around 25 restaurants offering a wide range of Asian and Western cuisines. The place is geared to the tourist trade and you will find reasonable prices and English-speaking waiters here.

Fung Ping Shan Museum: See MUSEUMS.

Government House: Upper Albert Rd, Central, Hong Kong. Dating from 1855, this is the official residence of Hong Kong's governors. During World War II it was occupied by the Japanese Army, and the building was remodelled and partly rebuilt with the addition of the central pagoda-like tower. It is not open to the public.

Guangzhou: Principal city of China's Guangdong province, Guangzhou lies on the banks of the Pearl River about 250 km north of Hong Kong. It is one of the oldest cities in China and for over a thousand years has been the gateway for foreign trade. Its proximity to Hong Kong has made it the most Westernized and capitalistic of the country's cities, and one of the least typical, however this does not detract from its popularity as a destination for travellers. Prospective visitors must first have a visa, which can be obtained by taking passport-size photographs to any travel agent or to the China Travel Service (CTS) office at 77 Queen's Rd, Central, Hong Kong, tel: 5-259121 or 27 Nathan Rd, Tsim Sha Tsui, Kowloon, tel: 3-667201. It costs HK$70-100 and takes 48 hours (visas can be had in 24 hours, but this costs extra at around HK$200-250). You can then travel to Guangzhou on an organized tour (contact the HKTA – see **Tourist Information**), or independently (see **EXCURSION 3**): there are three express trains daily from Hung Hom Terminus in Kowloon (HK$190 one-way, takes about two and a half hours). The Pearl River Shipping Company also operates a daily ferry service between the China Ferry Terminal in Kowloon and the Zhoutouzi Wharf in Guangzhou. There are two ships, M.V. Xinghu and M.V. Tianhu, and one leaves HK and the other leaves Guangzhou each night at 2100, arriving at their destinations at around 0700 the following morning. One-way tickets cost around HK$150 for a bunk in a shared cabin, and can be purchased at Zhoutouzi Wharf in Guangzhou and at CTS offices and travel agents in Hong Kong.

Guides: See **Tours**.

Hakka People: This matriarchal Chinese farming tribe, known as the 'guest people' because they migrated here from the north of China hundreds of years ago, inhabits many villages in the New Territories, and its members can be identified easily by their black, pyjama-like clothing and the wide-brimmed, black-fringed, hats worn by the women. You will see them in the walled villages of Kam Tin (see **EXCURSION 1**) where you will be expected to cough up a couple of dollars to take photographs of them.

Happy Valley: The flattest piece of land on Hong Kong Island, the valley was one of the first areas to be settled in the early 1840s, but was soon abandoned when it was found to be infested with malaria-carrying mosquitoes. The area was drained in 1845 and soon became the site of the colony's first race course. Horse racing has since become Hong Kong's chief passion and today's modern race course draws crowds of 35,000. It is estimated that as much money is gambled in one afternoon here as at all the race courses in Britain added together! See **WALK 3** .

Health: Hong Kong possesses top-quality medical facilities and most hotels have their own English-speaking doctor on call. In an emergency, dial 999 and ask for an ambulance. There is no free health service, so ensure that you arrange adequate medical insurance before your trip. The following hospitals have 24-hour casualty departments:
Queen Mary Hospital, Pok Fu Lam Rd, Pok Fu Lam, Hong Kong, tel: 5-8192111.
Queen Elizabeth Hospital, Wylie Rd, King's Park, Kowloon, tel: 3-7102111.
If you find yourself in need of dental treatment your hotel should be able to recommend a good dentist. Alternatively, consult the Business Telephone Directory under Dental Surgeons.
Hong Kong is free of malaria and other tropical diseases, so vaccinations are not required unless you intend to visit other, affected, areas of South East Asia. But remember to take precautions against the effects of sun and heat however, by using a sun hat and blocking cream, drinking plenty of fluids, and taking extra salt. If the heat does get too much for you, you can always take refuge in the air-conditioned, cool atmosphere of one of the hotels or shopping centres. See **Disabled People**, **Emergency Numbers**, **Insurance**.

Hollywood Road: See WALK 2.

Hong Kong Museum of History: See MUSEUMS.

Hong Kong Space Museum: See CHILDREN.

Hongkong and Shanghai Bank Building: This dramatic building on Des Voeux Rd, Central, Hong Kong, was opened in 1986 and designed by the British architect Norman Foster, and is thought to be the world's most expensive building (US$1 billion!). The floors of the 185 m-high structure are hung, in the manner of a supension bridge, from cylindrical steel towers, and are connected by a series of escalators. The lower part of the building is occupied by a 50 m-high atrium, and the bronze lion statues from the previous bank building (complete with wartime bullet marks) stand outside on the pavement.

Immaculate Conception Cathedral: Hong Kong's Roman Catholic cathedral at 16 Caine Rd, Central, Hong Kong, dates from 1888 when it replaced the original cathedral which had burnt down twice. The present building seats over 4000 people and has beautiful stained glass windows made more than 80 years ago in Toulouse. It contains fine Italian-made altars salvaged from the old cathedral.

Insurance: You are strongly advised to take out adequate travel and medical insurance before your trip. Your travel agent should be able to recommend a suitable policy. See **Crime & Theft**, **Driving**, **Health**.

Jade Market: See MARKETS.

Jamia Masjid: Hong Kong's modern mosque and Islamic Centre, completed in 1984, is situated on Nathan Road next to Kowloon Park (see **PARKS & GARDENS**). The white, marble-domed building with its four minarets serves the colony's 50,000-strong Moslem community.

Jardine House: Formerly known as the Connaught Centre, and sited on Connaught Rd, Central, Hong Kong, this is the headquarters of the old Hong Kong merchant company of Jardine. Built in 1972, it is one of the most easily recognizable of Hong Kong's skyscrapers – a grey, 52-storey tower next door to the Star Ferry terminal, pierced by 1748 circular windows (the local Chinese people have nicknamed it the 'House of a Thousand Arseholes'). You will find the General Post Office and the Government Publications Centre at its foot.

Kam Tin Walled Villages: See EXCURSION 1.

Kennedy Town: This district lies at the end of the Hong Kong's tram system's line, and is the colony's oldest and most traditional Chinese residential and commercial area. The waterfront, crowded with junks and lighters, is a bustle of loading and unloading, and the streets are lined with traditional shops and markets.

KCR (Kowloon to Canton Railway): The KCR links Hong Kong to the mainland Chinese rail network, and through that to the USSR and Europe. The line connects the Hung Hom terminus in Kowloon to the Chinese city of Guangzhou (see EXCURSION 3, A-Z). The stretch of line within Hong Kong is also a busy commuter link between Kowloon and the New Territories. Trains run between Hung Hom and Sheung Shui (as far as you can go without a visa for China) every three to 20 minutes (0545-2400; single fare HK$2.00-5.40) and the ticketing system is the same as for the MTR (see A-Z). For more information, tel: 0-6069600. See **MTR**, **Transport**.

Ladder Street: See WALK 2.

Lamma: See Outlying Islands.

Landmark, The: See SHOPPING 2.

Lan Kwai Fong: See Nightlife.

Lantau: See Outlying Islands.

Lau Fau Shan: See EXCURSION 1.

Laundries: Most hotels provide an efficient, if expensive, laundry service. There are many Chinese laundries in Tsim Sha Tsui, where you can have your washing done in a couple of hours for HK$20 or less. Look in the Business Telephone Directory under Launderers.

Legislative Council Building: This granite building on Jackson Rd, Central, Hong Kong, was formerly the home of the Supreme Court before it moved to new premises in Queensway in 1984. Construction was completed in 1910 and the building, with its arched colonnades, is an attractive example of colonial architecture (one of the few remaining examples in Hong Kong). A statue of blindfolded Justice still stands above the main portico and overlooks Statue Square. The building is now home to the 56-member Legislative Council (known as Legco) which forms the middle tier of Hong Kong's administration and passes laws to effect policies decided by the 21-member Executive Council.

Lei Yue Mun: This collection of fishing villages, lying along the north side of the eastern harbour entrance, is justly famed for its seafood restaurants. Choose your meal from the fish markets or from the restaurants' own tanks, and enjoy it steamed, fried, grilled or baked. You can get here by ferry and sampan from Sai Wan Ho pier (MTR Sai Wan Ho, or tram to Shau Kei Wan), or by bus 14C from MTR Kwun Tong.

Li Yuen Streets East & West: See MARKETS (THE LANES).

Lok Ma Chau: See EXCURSION 1.

Lost Property: Report any loss to your hotel and/or to the police, tel: 5-284284, ext. 484.

Luk Yu Teahouse: Built in the 1930s and relocated to its present site at 24-26 Stanley St, Central, Hong Kong in 1975, the Luk Yu is one of Hong Kong's few remaining traditional teahouses (open 0700-2200).

It is a place to meet friends for a chat or to clinch a business deal. The handsome carved wooden doors, hardwood panelling, marble facings, brass spittoons, wooden facade and calligraphic sign were all brought from the original site. The Luk Yu serves a range of Chinese teas and dim sum snacks, and gets very busy between 1200-1330. The waiters are renowned for their aloofness towards foreigners, but it is still worth a visit to soak up the authentic atmosphere.

Macau: Founded in 1557 as a Portuguese trading post, Macau today thrives on tourism and gambling. Sometimes called the Las Vegas of the East (something of an overstatement), Macau's six casinos draw thousands of Hong Kong residents every night and weekend (except for horse racing, gambling is illegal in Hong Kong). But for the traveller, it is Macau's historical sights and unique blend of Mediterranean and Oriental cultures that provide the main interest (see **EXCURSION 2**). Macau lies 65 km west of Hong Kong across the Pearl River estuary and is easily reached by ferry, hydrofoil or jetfoil. Visas are not required for UK, Commonwealth, USA and most European citizens. Most sailings depart from the Macau Ferry terminal beside the Shun Tak Centre (MTR Sheung Wan, or ten minute walk from Central). The fastest way to Macau is by jetfoil, a 45-minute trip with departures at least every 30 minutes between 0700-1830, and less frequent between 1830-0700. Return fares range from HK$130-190 depending on the time of travel. For more information contact the Macau Tourist Information Board office in the Shun Tak Centre (see **SHOPPING 2**), tel: 5-408198 (0900-1700 Mon.-Fri., 0900-1300 Sat). See **EXCURSION 2**.

Man Fat Sze Temple (Temple of 10,000 Buddhas): This is actually a complex of five temples built (in the 1950s) on the hillside above the new town of Sha Tin in the New Territories. From the Sha Tin KCR (see **A-Z**) station, follow the signposts to the steep path leading up to the temple. Halfway up on the right is the small Thai-style Fat Wah Temple. The steps beyond lead to the main temple, with its famous 12,800 figures of the Buddha (each 30 cm high), and a nine-storey pagoda. Beyond are four smaller temples, the rightmost of which houses the embalmed and gilded body of Yuet Kai, the monk who founded the temple. See **MUSTS, TEMPLES**.

Man Mo Temple: This popular temple is as old as the colony, and is dedicated to two deities: Man Cheung, god of literature and patron of civil servants, who represents the virtues of the statesman (Man); and Kwan Tung, god of war and patron of pawnbrokers, the police, the military and curio dealers, who represents the virtues of the soldier (Mo). Inside, past the *dong chung*, a red carved screen which keeps evil spirits out, is the smoke tower, hung with coils of burning incense which carry prayers up to heaven. To the left are three antique sedan chairs, which were used to carry the images of Man and Mo through the streets during festivals. Opposite these are the temple drum and bell (cast in China in 1847). In the Main Hall beyond, hung with lanterns and fragrant with incense, you will find three splendid wooden altars; the main altar carries the statues of Man (on the right, in red robes) and Mo (on the left, in green robes). See **TEMPLES**.

Man Wa Lane: See **WALK 2**.

Maxicabs: See Buses.

Mid Levels: See CITY DISTRICTS.

Minibuses: See Buses.

Money: Banking hours are 0900-1630 Mon.-Fri., 0900-1230 Sat. Foreign currency and traveller's cheques can be exchanged at banks, hotels and licensed moneychangers, but banks give the best rates of exchange. Moneychangers are open during shopping hours and advertise attractive rates, however their commission makes them a worse deal than the banks. Try not to change any money at the airport moneychangers as it has the worst rates in the colony. You will need your passport to change traveller's cheques. Major credit and charge cards are widely accepted and Visa cardholders can also obtain local currency from the Hongkong Bank 'Electronic Money' automatic teller machines at the airport and in the city. If you lose traveller's cheques or credit cards, inform the police immediately (tel: 999) and contact the issuing company. The American Express Travel Service office is at New

World Tower, 16-18 Queen's Rd, Central, Hong Kong, tel: 5-8431888.
See **Currency**.

MTR (Mass Transit Railway): The MTR is Hong Kong's modern,
efficient and easy-to-use underground railway system. Air-conditioned
trains run on three interconnected lines: the Island Line (along the north
side of Hong Kong from Sheung Wan through Central to Chai Wan); the
Tsuen Wan Line (from Central under the harbour to Kowloon and on to
Tsuen Wan); and the Kwun Tong Line (from Yau Ma Tei east to Kwun
Tong). Kowloon Tong station on the Kwun Tong line has an interchange
with the KCR (see **A-Z**). Trains run every five minutes from 0600-0100.
Fares range from HK$2.50-6.00. Find out the fare to your destination
from the list beside the ticket machines, then buy a ticket for that
amount (only single tickets can be purchased). Ticket machines in stations accept HK$1, 2, 5 and 50 and 20c coins (you can change notes at
the station Information Desks). The ticket allows you to pass through an
electronic turnstile onto the platforms. Hang on to it as you will also
need it to exit at your destination. Tickets are valid for the day of purchase only and expire 90 minutes after you pass through the turnstile
(to deter joyriders). A free copy of the MTR Guidebook, containing
maps and timetables, and listing fares and connecting bus services, is
available from station Information Desks. A special Tourist Ticket
(HK$20) can be bought at HKTA (see **Tourist Information**) offices and
all MTR and KCR (see **A-Z**) booking offices. It must be purchased within 14 days of your arrival in Hong Kong and you must present your
passport as proof of visitor status. It works just like an ordinary ticket,
but gives HK$20 worth of travel on all MTR and KCR trains, and is
returned to you at the exit turnstile each time you make a journey (the
electronic turnstile having deducted the cost of the trip from the value
remaining on your ticket). As a bonus, on your last journey you can
travel anywhere on the MTR/KCR network no matter how little value
remains on the ticket. For more information, tel: 5-250557.
See **Transport**.

Music: Traditional Chinese music can be heard daily at the Cultural
Shows staged by the HKTA (see **Tourist Information**), which feature

classical music, opera, puppet theatre, folk songs and dances etc. There are also weekly shows at the New World Centre and the City Plaza (see **SHOPPING 2**), and more daily shows at the Empire Centre, Moody Rd, Tsim Sha Tsui East. For information on times and details tel: 3-7225555. The Hong Kong Chinese Orchestra also gives performances of traditional Chinese music (tel: 3-348465) and regular classical concerts are performed by the Hong Kong Philharmonic Orchestra at City Hall from Sept.-June (see **ENTERTAINMENT**).

In addition, there are lunchtime concerts at St John's Cathedral on Wednesdays between 1320-1400.

Live jazz and rock music can be heard at a number of pubs and clubs in the city. For more information, check local newspapers or contact the HKTA (see **ENTERTAINMENT**, **NIGHTLIFE**, **What's On**.

New Territories: The largest part of Hong Kong lies between Kowloon and the Chinese border, about 25 km to the north. This area is called the New Territories, and was leased to Great Britain for 99 years under the second Convention Of Peking in 1898 (Hong Kong Island and Kowloon were ceded in perpetuity, but as they could not function without the hinterland of the New Territories they too will be returned to China in 1997). The area reveals a side of Hong Kong that is missed by most tourists, and is well worth taking at least a day to explore its traditional market towns, like Yuen Wo, its fishing communities, like Lau Fau Shan, its new towns, like Sha Tin and Yuen Long, and its large expanses of unspoilt scenic countryside (see Sai Kung Peninsula). See **EXCURSION 1**.

Newspapers: There are two local English-language daily newspapers: the staid *South China Morning Post* and the more radical *Hong Kong Standard*, each costing HK$3.00. The *Asian Wall Street Journal* and the *International Herald Tribune* are also published here. The weekly news magazines *Asiaweek, Far Eastern Economic Review, Time* and *Newsweek* are all widely available. British newspapers can be had, a few days late, at most city newsagents and bookshops. The cheapest place to buy them is at the Kowloon Star Ferry Terminal. See **What's On**.

Nightlife: Hong Kong's varied and lively nightlife includes cocktail lounges, Chinese and Western-style nightclubs, discos, jazz clubs, pubs, hostess clubs and topless bars. Because many people work long hours and Saturday mornings, nightspots tend to fill up late in the evening, and Saturday rather than Friday is the big night out.
The Lan Kwai Fong area in Central (between D'Aguilar Street and Wyndham Street) has a number of sophisticated wine bars and discos patronized by a chic blend of expats and young Chinese. British-style pubs offering draught Bass and darts can be found in Central and Wan Chai, while shades of Suzie Wong haunt the slightly sleazy topless bars of Tsim Sha Tsui's Peking, Lock and Hankow Roads. See CITY DISTRICTS.
Discos are large, loud and very popular with local youngsters. They open their doors around 2100-2230 and close at 0200-0300, and you can expect a cover charge of about HK$100 (includes two drinks). The elegant and glitzy Japanese-style hostess clubs are strictly for the affluent businessman and occasional well-off tourist – spend even one hour in one of these clubs and you could easily be HK$500 the poorer! Club Volvo, Lower G/F Mandarin Palace, 14 Science Museum Rd, Tsim Sha Tsui East, Kowloon, is the world's largest Japanese-style nightclub (1500-0400; min. admission HK$150 including two drinks, table HK$150 per hr, hostess HK$40 for 15 min).
The HKTA (see **Tourist Information**) publishes a useful 'Nightlife' guide, and offers an unescorted 'Night On The Town' tour, complete with itinerary and coupons, to give the visitor a taste of selected nightspots. See ENTERTAINMENT, NIGHTLIFE.

Noonday Gun: Situated in a small waterfront garden opposite the Excelsior Hotel in Causeway Bay (see CITY DISTRICTS), this three-pound Hotchkiss gun, made in 1901, is fired each day on the stroke of noon, continuing a tradition begun in the 19thC by the great Hong Kong merchants, Jardine Matheson. The ceremony is immortalized in the words of the Noel Coward song Mad Dogs And Englishmen:
'… in Hong Kong they strike a gong, and fire off a noonday gun …'.
The only other occasion it is fired is at midnight on New Year's Eve.

Ocean Park: See CHILDREN.

Ohel Leah Synagogue: Built in 1902 by Sir Jacob Sassoon to honour his mother Leah, this is Hong Kong's only synagogue. It is notable for its architecture which derives from Dutch colonial style. Open 0600-2100 Mon.-Sat; services 1830 Fri., 0900 Sat.

Opening Times:
Banks – 0900-1630 Mon.-Fri., 0900-1230 Sat.
Offices – 0900-1300, 1400-1730 Mon.-Fri., 0900-1300 Sat.
Post Offices – 0900-1700 Mon.-Fri., 0900-1300 Sat.
Restaurants – 1200-1500, 1800-2300.
Shops – 1000-2130.

Orientation: Hong Kong consists of a peninsula and numerous islands, lying on the east side of the Pearl River estuary, south of China's Guangdong province. The colony is 48 km north to south, and 65 km east to west and largely mountainous. The city centre is on the north shore of Hong Kong Island and on the mainland peninsula of Kowloon, the two parts being separated by Victoria Harbour. The rest of the islands, and the New Territories extending north from Kowloon to the Chinese border, are largely rural, interrupted by the apartment blocks of new towns. Maps of Hong Kong are available from the HKTA (see **Tourist Information**). Addresses of shops and offices in tower blocks often take the following form e.g. 3/F New World Tower, which means 'third floor'. Ground floor is G/F and basement is B/F. When Hong Kong appears in an address in the TOPICS section of this book, it has been abbreviated to HK. See CITY DISTRICTS, **Outlying Islands**.

Outlying Islands: Hong Kong has more than 230 islands, mostly uninhabited. Three to visit are: Lantau, the largest, twice as big as Hong Kong Island, but sparsely populated, attractions include Po Lin Monastery (see TEMPLES, **A-Z**), the Lantau Tea Gardens, the village of Tai O; Cheung Chau with seven temples, including the ancient Pak Tai Temple (see TEMPLES), charming narrow streets, and the Bun Festival (see **Events**); and Lamma which has a Tin Hau Temple, lovely walks and seafood restaurants. These islands are reached by ferry. For information and timetables, contact the HKTA (see **Tourist Information**).

Parking: It is usually impossible to find a space on working days. Rates in multi-storey car parks are around HK$5-15 per hour.

Passports & Customs: A valid passport is necessary, but no visa is required by UK citizens for stays of up to six months. Stays of up to three months are permitted without a visa for citizens of Commonwealth countries, and up to one month for citizens of the USA. A vaccination certificate for cholera is not required unless you have been in an affected area 14 days prior to your arrival. See **Customs Allowances**.

Peak, The: See CITY DISTRICTS, MUSTS, WALK 1.

Peak Tram: This was opened, on 30 May, 1888, by Governor Sir William Des Voeux to ease the journey from Central (see CITY DISTRICTS) to the mansions on The Peak. Before then transport to the upper levels of The Peak had been by sedan chair. The track is 1400 m long and carries two tram cars connected by a 1500 m steel cable; as one car descends, it pulls the other one up. Halfway up the trams pass each other. The trams run every ten minutes (0700-2400) from the lower terminus in Garden Road, Central, to Victoria Gap, with request stops at Kennedy Rd, Macdonnel Rd, Bowen Rd, May Rd and Barker Rd. The journey time is eight minutes and the one-way fare is HK$6.00, child HK$2.00 (return HK$10.00, child HK$4.00). There is a free shuttle bus between the Star Ferry terminal, via Central MTR station (Chater Rd exit), and the lower terminus (0900-1900). See MUSTS, **Transport**.

Police: Hong Kong police wear khaki uniforms and are generally polite and helpful to visitors. Officers with a red flash under their shoulder badge speak English. In an emergency, dial 999 and ask for the police. To report a crime, use the Crime Hotline on 5-277177. For other more general enquiries, tel: 5-284284, ext 484. See **Crime & Theft**, **Emergency Numbers**.

Po Lin (Precious Lotus) Monastery: This Buddhist monastery is situated on a plateau beneath Lantau Peak on Lantau Island. Standing beside the gates is the largest figure of a Buddha in South East Asia, a

34 m-high, copper-sheathed statue that cost HK$60 million. The monastery has up to 2000 visitors each day, and over 10,000 on the festival of Lord Sakyamuni Buddha's birthday (mid-May). Many people come to spend a night in the dormitory accommodation (around HK$80 including three vegetarian meals) and rise early to climb Lantau Peak (934 m) to watch the sunrise from its summit. See **TEMPLES**.

Possession Street: See **WALK 2**.

Post Offices: The two General Post Offices are at 2 Connaught Pl., Central (beside Star Ferry Terminal), Hong Kong, and at 405 Nathan Rd, Yau Ma Tei, Kowloon. These offices are open 0800-1800 Mon.-Sat. and offer letter, parcel, fax and poste restante services. Letters addressed c/o Poste Restante, Hong Kong, go to the Central office. Postcards and air-mail letters to the UK weighing under 10g cost HK$1.80, plus HK$0.90 for each additional gram, and aerogrammes are HK$1.40. If you have enquiries on any postal matter, tel: 5-231071 or 3-7808598 (0900-1700 Mon.-Fri.).

Public Holidays: New Year's Day (1 Jan.); Chinese New Year (three days in late Jan./early Feb); Ching Ming Festival (April); Good Friday, Easter Saturday & Easter Monday; Dragon Boat Festival (May/June); HM Queen's Birthday (14 June); Liberation Day (last Sat. & Mon. in Aug.); Mooncake Festival (Sep.); Chung Yeung Festival (Oct.); Christmas Day & Boxing Day (25-26 Dec.). See **Events**.

Railways: See **KCR, MTR**.

Religious Services:
Anglican – St John's Cathedral, Garden Rd, Central, Hong Kong, tel: 5-234157.
Jewish – Ohel Leah Synagogue, 70 Robinson Rd, Mid Levels, Hong Kong, tel: 5-594821.
Methodist – 271 Queen's Rd East, Central, Hong Kong, tel: 5-757817.
Roman Catholic – St Joseph's, 7 Garden Rd, Central, Hong Kong, tel: 5-252629.

Repulse Bay: Repulse Bay on the south side of Hong Kong Island is Hong Kong's most popular beach. It should be avoided on sunny weekends when you can hardly see the sand for bodies, but is a pleasant spot during the week. There are lifeguards, showers, changing rooms, and a huge Macdonald's fast-food restaurant. The Life Guard Club is built in Chinese style and decorated with two huge statues of Tin Hau and Kwun Yum, the protectors of fisherfolk. See **CHILDREN**, **SPORTS**.

Rickshaws: This form of transport, dating from the 1870s, has all but died out, and remains as a tourist attraction only. The ageing rickshaw 'boys' would be flabbergasted if you asked them to go further than a quick spin round the block (most tourists settle for a photograph). The rickshaw boys congregate around the Star Ferry Terminal in Central (see **CITY DISTRICTS**). You must haggle a price, but expect to pay HK$50-100 for a five-minute ride and HK$20-50 for a photograph.

St John's Cathedral: The colony's Gothic-style Anglican cathedral, on Garden Rd, Central, Hong Kong, was completed in 1849 and is one of the oldest in Asia. The wooden doors are fashioned from timber taken from HMS *Tamar*, a stores depot ship that lay moored in Victoria Harbour from 1897 to 1941.

Shopping: There is everything from market stalls to modern shopping centres, backstreet businesses to designer boutiques.

Western, one of the main shopping areas, contains many traditional Chinese shops and businesses where you can buy all kinds of Chinese goods. Shops selling Asian antiques, crafts, curios and bric-a-brac can be found in the area of Hollywood Road and Cat Street, while Central boasts stylish shopping centres full of boutiques and leather shops, and is riddled with alleys packed with stalls selling clothes and textiles. In Wan Chai you can find traditional furniture shops down Queen's Road East and Wan Chai Road; and Causeway Bay has several Japanese department stores, plus the clothes market of Jardine's Bazaar. Across the harbour the streets around Tsim Sha Tsui's Nathan Road are crammed with shops selling cameras, hi-fis, jewellery, electronics, clothes and souvenirs. Factory outlets in the Hung Hom district offer clothes and jewellery at near wholesale prices. But before you plunge into the fray do some homework: get hold of the HKTA's (see **Tourist Information**) *Official Guide to Shopping and Eating Out* which is full of excellent advice and contains a comprehensive list of approved outlets. Shop around and compare prices (not only between shops, but against those back home as some things, especially cameras, may not be the bargains you expect). Deal only with reputable establishments, such as those listed by the HKTA which display the HKTA's junk symbol in their windows and can be relied upon to be helpful and informative, as well as giving value for money. Department stores always have fixed prices, but elsewhere it is worth asking for a discount, especially if you are buying several items at once.

Always ask for a receipt and a guarantee. Most shops that deal in bulky or fragile items will arrange to have your purchases shipped home, but ask how much extra this will cost. Shopping hours are generally 1000-1800 in Central, and 1000-2100 in Tsim Sha Tsui, Causeway Bay and Wan Chai. Most shops are open seven days a week, but some stores close on Sundays. The majority of shops close down over Chinese New Year (see **Events**). See **SHOPPING**, **Best Buys**, **Touts**.

Smoking: Smoking is forbidden in MTR trains and stations. European and American brands of cigarettes are on sale in shops and kiosks all

Sports: Details of sporting events in the colony can be obtained from the Sporting Promotion Programme, Queen Elizabeth Stadium, 18 Oi Kwan Rd, Wan Chai, Hong Kong, tel: 5-576793.

Golf – Royal Hong Kong Golf Club – see **SPORTS**. The Hong Kong Open is held here in late February. See **Clearwater Bay**.

Horse racing – Royal Hong Kong Jockey Club courses at Happy Valley, Hong Kong, and Sha Tin, New Territories. The season is Sept.-May and races are run on Wednesday evenings, Saturday afternoons and occasionally on Sundays too. Tourists can buy a badge for entry to the

Members' Stand for HK$50 on presentation of a passport. Alternatively, the HKTA (see **Tourist Information**) offers a tour package that includes a meal, transport and guide service for HK$250. For details contact the HKTA, tel: 5-244191.

Motor racing – The Macau Grand Prix takes place in late Nov., and is a mere 45-minute jetfoil ride from Hong Kong. For details, contact the Macau Tourist Information Board, tel: 3-677747.

Rugby Union – The international Rugby Sevens competition is held here each year at Easter. For details, contact the Hong Kong Rugby Football Union, Room 1401 Block A, Watson's Estate, 4-6 Watson's Rd, North Point, Hong Kong, tel: 5-660719. See **SPORTS**.

Sung Dynasty Village: This re-creation of a Chinese village from the Sung Dynasty (AD 960-1279) was built by a Hong Kong businessman on Lai Wan Rd, Lai Chi Kok, Kowloon. Its inhabitants wear period costumes and play the parts of craftsmen, blacksmiths, fortune tellers, wood carvers, dancers, acrobats and so on. At the Restaurant of Plentiful Joy in the village you can have a traditional meal while being entertained by folk musicians. It is possible to visit the village as part of an organized tour (Mon.-Fri.; HK$170-220 including transport and a meal) or independently (1230-1700 weekends & hol. only; admission HK$50/30). Contact the HKTA (see **Tourist Information**).

Taxis: Taxis are relatively inexpensive and convenient, except between 1600 and 1900 or on race days and rainy days when it is difficult to find one free. They are usually red (in the New Territories they are green) with a prominent TAXI sign on the roof, which is lit up when the taxi is for hire. They can be hailed in the street, picked up at a rank, or ordered by telephone. Most drivers speak a little English, but it is a wise move to get your hotel to write down your destination for you in Chinese. All taxis are metered: the flagfall is HK$6.50, plus HK$0.80 for every 250 m. There are surcharges for trips through the Cross-harbour Tunnel (HK$20) or Aberdeen Tunnel (HK$3); for each piece of luggage (HK$2); for waiting time (HK$0.80 per minute); and for a radio call (HK$1.00). See **Complaints**, **Tipping**, **Transport**.

Telephones & Telegrams: Local calls from private telephones are free. Public pay phones are rather scarce, but it is normal practice to nip into shops and restaurants and ask to use their phone. Local calls on pay phones cost HK$1.00. International Direct Dialling (IDD) calls can be made from hotel phones, Cable & Wireless offices, IDD Coinphones (which accept HK$1, 2 and 5 coins) and Cardphones (cards worth HK$50, 100 and 250 can be bought at Cable & Wireless offices). Coinphones and Cardphones can be found at the airport and at Star Ferry terminals. To make an IDD call, first dial 100 then the country code (44 for UK, 1 for USA), then the area code (without the initial zero), then the number. The cost of an IDD call to the UK is HK$10.50 per minute.

Directory enquiries	tel: 108
IDD enquiries	tel: 013
International operator	tel: 010
International collect calls	tel: 011

Telegrams, telexes and faxes can be sent from the two 24-hr Cable & Wireless offices at Room 1028, 1/F Exchange Square, Connaught Rd, Central, Hong Kong, and at Hermes House, 10 Middle Rd, Tsim Sha Tsui, Kowloon. There are many other offices throughout Hong Kong, but only these two offer a fax service. IDD calls can also be made from these offices: you pay a deposit, make your call, then pay for the time used at the end.

Television & Radio: Hong Kong has two English-language television channels (ATV and TVB, both commercial) which broadcast a selection of British, Australian, American and locally-made programmes, including regular international news bulletins.
There are three English-language radio stations: RTHK 3 (567kHz), RTHK 4 (91MHz and 100MHz) and Commercial Radio (1044kHz). The BBC World Service is relayed on 96MHz and 105MHz (06000-0645, 1700-0230).

Temple of 10,000 Buddhas: See **Man Fat Sze Temple**.

Temple Street Night Market: See MARKETS, MUSTS.

Tiger Balm (Aw Boon Haw) Gardens : See CHILDREN, PARKS & GARDENS.

Time Differences: Eight hours ahead of GMT all year round.

Tipping: Hotels and restaurants generally add a 10% service charge onto the bill, but a tip of 5-10% is also customary. Hotel porters expect around HK$3 per bag, tourist guides a tip of 5-10%, toilet attendants HK$1-2, and while taxi drivers do not always expect a tip, it is customary for the passenger to round the fare up to the next whole dollar (also give a tip of 5-10% if your taxi driver has been helpful).

Toilets: Public toilets are plentiful, but often unpleasant. Clean public toilets can be found in hotels and most shopping centres. Tip the attendant. There are no public toilets in MTR (see **A-Z**) stations. See **Tipping**.

Tourist Information: The Hong Kong Tourist Association (HKTA) issues the monthly *Hong Kong Official Guide* (HK$15) as well as many free booklets and fact sheets packed with useful advice and information, and maps. The friendly English-speaking staff will provide assis-

tance with sightseeing tours, bus and ferry schedules, and walking tours. There are HKTA offices at 35/F Jardine House (formerly Connaught Centre), Connaught Rd, Central, Hong Kong (0900-1800 Mon.-Fri., 0900-1300 Sat.-Sun.); at the Star Ferry Concourse, Tsim Sha Tsui, Kowloon (0800-1800 daily); and at the Royal Garden Hotel (G/F), Shop G2, 69 Mody Rd, Tsim Sha Tsui East, Kowloon (0800-1800 Mon.-Fri., 0800-1300 Sat.).

For general tourist information, tel: 3-7225555 (0800-1800 daily). For shopping advice, tel: 5-244191 ext 278, 0900-1700 Mon.-Fri., 0900-1300 Sat. The HKTA's UK office is on the 5th floor, 125 Pall Mall, London SW1Y 5EA, tel: 071-930 4775. See **Accommodation**, **Tours**, **What's On**.

Tours: There are more than 30 organized tours covering all areas and aspects of Hong Kong, from a 20-minute sampan tour of Aberdeen Typhoon Shelter, to a half-day tour of Hong Kong Island or a full day trip around the New Territories. Specialist tours cover horse-racing, the islands, nightlife, and more. Prices range from HK$40 to over HK$700, and full details are contained in the HKTA's sightseeing booklet (see **Tourist Information**).

Trams: Hong Kong's tram system has been in operation since 1904, though the trams now in use were built in the 1950s and 60s. The trams run along the north side of Hong Kong Island from Kennedy Town in the west to Shau Kei Wan, with a loop around Happy Valley, every few minutes (0540-0100), and there is a flat fare of 60c (child 20c). Destinations are marked on the front of the tram and you enter at the rear and exit at the front, paying the exact fare into a box beside the driver on your way out. See **MUSTS**, **Peak Tram**, **Transport**.

Transport: Hong Kong's public transport is generally fast, inexpensive, easy to use, and remarkably varied. A combination of the Star Ferry and the MTR is the best way to move between the city areas, and walking is best for exploring the streets and shops of Western, Central and Kowloon (see **CITY DISTRICTS**). For exploring further afield, you can use buses, the KCR, ferries and taxis. Every visitor should take the opportunity to travel on a Hong Kong tram and ride on the Peak Tram funicular railway. Avoid rush-hour travel. Hong Kong is connected by daily, air-conditioned express trains to Guangzhou in China (see **EXCURSION 3**, **A–Z**), and by daily ferries and hydrofoils to Guangzhou and Macau (see **EXCURSION 2**, **A–Z**).
See **Airport**, **Buses**, **Driving**, **Ferries**, **KCR**, **MTR**, **Peak Tram**, **Taxis**, **Trams**, **Walla-wallas**.

Traveller's Cheques: See **Money**.

Tsim Sha Tsui: See **CITY DISTRICTS**.

Walla-wallas: This is the local name for the small, motorized water taxis that ply back and forth across the harbour 24 hours a day. They are available at Queen's Pier (immediately east of the Star Ferry terminal), Central, and at the Star Ferry pier, Kowloon, and can be useful late at night when you have missed the last Star Ferry. Fares are around HK$8 per person or HK$60-70 for the whole boat. See **Transport**.

Wan Chai: See CITY DISTRICTS, WALK 3.

Water World: See CHILDREN.

Western District: See CITY DISTRICTS, WALK 2.

What's On: In addition to the local press, the following publications are useful sources of information: the weekly *Hong Kong Visitors' Newspaper* which is free from HKTA (see **Tourist Information**) and hotels and covers tourist attractions, shopping, restaurants and nightlife; the weekly *Television & Entertainment Times* costing HK$6.00 from newsagents; the monthly *City News* which can be obtained for free from City Hall and the HK Arts Centre, and lists coming cultural and sporting events (there is also a free monthly *Programme Diary* listing events at the HK Arts Centre and the HK Academy of Performing Arts); and the monthly *Official Hong Kong Guide* costing HK$15.00 from the HKTA (or free from hotels) and full of useful information, including sporting events and festivals. See **Events**, **Newspapers**.

Wong Tai Sin Temple: Although built in traditional style, this temple dates from 1973. It is dedicated to the god Wong Tai Sin, introduced to Hong Kong in 1915, for whom a temple was first built in 1921. This original temple was demolished in the 1960s and replaced by the present building. Wong Tai Sin is reputed to have the power to cure sickness and give advice about the future – hence the large numbers who flock here for horse-racing tips! The alley leading to the temple is crowded with fortune-tellers, palm readers, and stalls selling incense, oranges (as food offerings), and the little plastic windmills Chinese gods seem to be very fond of. See TEMPLES.

Yau Ma Tei: See CITY DISTRICTS.

Youth Hostels: There are eight IYHA youth hostels in Hong Kong, most of which are situated in remote rural areas. The YHA Head Office is in Room 1408 Block A, Watson's Estate, 4-6 Watson's Rd, North Point, Hong Kong, tel: 5-700985. If you are not a member, you can join

here for HK$80. It costs HK$8 a night for a bed in one of the hostels (which are closed during the day between 1000-1600). Ma Wui Hall YH, Mount Davis Path, Mount Davis, tel: 5-875715 is in a lovely setting above Kennedy Town (see **A-Z**) at the west end of Hong Kong Island. The other hostels are on Lantau Island (see **Outlying Islands**) and in the New Territories (see **A-Z**). See **Accommodation**.

Zoological & Botanical Gardens: See CHILDREN, PARKS & GARDENS.